GW00789358

THE CHALLENGE OF OUTSOURCING HUMAN RESOURCES

CHANDOS BUSINESS GUIDES
HUMAN RESOURCES & TRAINING

Chandos Business Guides are designed to provide managers with practical, down-to-earth information. The Chandos Business Guides are written by leading authors in their respective fields. If you would like to receive a full listing of current and forthcoming titles, please visit our web site www.chandospublishing.com or contact Melinda Taylor on email mtaylor@chandospublishing.com or direct telephone number +44 (0) 1865 882727.

New authors: we are always pleased to receive ideas for new titles; if you would like to write a Chandos Business Guide, please contact Dr Glyn Jones on email gjones@chandospublishing.com or direct telephone number +44 (0) 1865 884447.

Bulk orders: some organisations buy a number of copies of our books. If you are interested in doing this, we would be pleased to discuss a discount. Please contact Dr Glyn Jones on email gjones@chandospublishing.com or direct telephone number +44 (0) 1865 884447.

THE CHALLENGE OF OUTSOURCING HUMAN RESOURCES

SALLY VANSON

Chandos Publishing

Oxford · England

Chandos Publishing (Oxford) Limited
Chandos House
5 & 6 Steadys Lane
Stanton Harcourt
Oxford OX8 1RL
England
Tel: +44 (0) 1865 882727 Fax: +44 (0) 1865 884448
Email: sales@chandospublishing.com
www.chandospublishing.com

••

First published in Great Britain in 2001

ISBN 1 902375 86 6

© S. Vanson, 2001

All rights reserved. No part of this publication may be reproduced, stored in or introduced into a retrieval system, or transmitted, in any form, or by any means (electronic, mechanical, photocopying, recording or otherwise) without the prior written permission of the Publishers. This publication may not be lent, resold, hired out or otherwise disposed of by way of trade in any form of binding or cover other than that in which it is published without the prior consent of the Publishers. Any person who does any unauthorised act in relation to this publication may be liable to criminal prosecution and civil claims for damages.

The Publishers make no representation, express or implied, with regard to the accuracy of the information contained in this publication and cannot accept any legal responsibility or liability for any errors or omissions.

The material contained in this publication constitutes general guidelines only and does not represent to be advice on any particular matter. No reader or purchaser should act on the basis of material contained in this publication without first taking professional advice appropriate to their particular circumstances. Readers of this publication should be aware that only Acts of Parliament and Statutory Instruments have the force of law and that only courts can authoritatively interpret the law.

Typeset by Turn-Around Typesetting
Printed by Biddles, Guildford, UK

Contents

Acknowledgements

This book is dedicated to my daughter Lucy, the most patient and understanding 11-year-old, one could hope for. Her creativity, interest, energy, flexibility, enthusiasm and motivation are something that many organisations could learn from.

My thanks also go to Charles Brook, my friend and business partner for his encouragement and support, his feedback on the initial manuscript and his unwaivering belief that the book would get written on time.

I also want to thank David Heslop for the learning and varying perspectives I have gained about organisations and corporate life while being employed in MCL Group and of course Claire Greenslade, for proofing and tidying the manuscript to ensure it met the publishing deadline.

No book is the product of the author alone, so finally I thank everyone who has been or is working with me, colleagues, clients, partners, fellow course delegates and tutors and my support team for whatever unconscious input they have given that has allowed my thinking to broaden, my ideas to be challenged and my learning to develop along the journey. This includes the authors of books and articles I have read in my life and courses I have attended. I believe that no ideas or concepts are unique, we all spin off each other at some stage, so thank you to fellow members of the human race for sharing and contributing the thought processes which enable information sharing and evolution.

Preface

Life in organisations is the endless study of the human race. If a Martian landed on Earth the key question s/he may ask is 'why do so many smart people do so many dumb things?' The answer – so they can have fun watching the world go round, and indeed it does. Outsourcing will be followed by in-sourcing and maybe even co-sourcing as surely as centralisation follows decentralisation. We are all on a continuous journey with no destination as far as the evolution of Human Resources is concerned and it is exactly that fact that makes it so exciting.

'Positive skills, attitudes and behaviour which enhance clearly understood relationships with every one we touch, and encourage their motivations to buy.' That is the holy grail of every commercial and many not-for-profit organisations. The current obsession with customer centricity as the only differentiator from the competition is one of the driving forces behind the outsourcing trend. *'An internet year is three months'* is a driving force behind the need to focus on core competences and outsource the peripheral work. In this race for supreme commercial performance everyone is a customer and the customer is king.

The Human Resources function is changing as you read this preface. No longer is it the old world of 'the company policeman', but rather an evolutionary strategy that adds the value and distinction that enables competition in a world where increased learning and information sharing is resulting in similarity and sanitisation of the corporate environment. Why, I ask myself, would anyone spend time looking at prehistoric absenteeism records as a justification for lack of productivity when they could be creating new patterns of working in a complex, chaotic and exciting future.

The new Human Resources activities focus around the exploration of the relationship between process and culture, between behaviour and commercial patterns and the whole is supported through flexibility.

The cultural maps in organisations symbolise the connections between the external world and the internal representations of the decision makers. They set the scope of responsibility with respect to individuals, employees, teams and the whole organisation. The cultural changes involved in outsourcing single or multiple activities should not be underestimated. Once change has happened the company can never return to yesterday, the dynamics have moved on.

This book suggests some important messages for outsource service providers who will need to match performance to service in terms of quality, effectiveness, efficiency and personal service, give total commitment to customers, develop people then use their expertise to seek better ways of doing things based on standards and targets, use of data and statistics to drive continuous improvement while combining the art of people management with science of reducing variability.

The book attempts to give an overview of the outsourcing strategy and discusses whether it is part of an overall plan or stands alone. It challenges the business case according to affordability and profitability. The elements that make up the HR function are reviewed with a look at the key considerations to take into account, before prompting thoughts about the choice of supplier, the proposal and tendering system and how to make informed decisions. Of prime importance to the author is the cultural fit, alignment of beliefs and values and the generation of behaviours on the part of client and provider to build a mutually trusting and inclusive partnership. Thoughts about these softer areas are shared before discussing the harder elements of the service level agreements, forming the contracts and the pricing structures. Like any change management process the outsourcing initiative would not be complete without recognising the need to manage the communication of the decision and the implementation plan. This is quickly followed by a view about managing the future and ensuring the sustainable strategic health of the outsourced activity for all concerned.

The major objective for the provider will be to improve customer focus to the point where client company performance is significantly superior to that offered by other trading companies, and thus adding value to themselves and their public profile along the journey.

Success criteria will include the need:

- to carry out primary research to establish client needs and expectations and to redefine at least annually;

- to set a clear common purpose;

- to use client data to set service standards;

- to offer all employees regular awareness programmes;

- to maintain customer orientated teams and tap potential at all levels of the supplier organisation;

- to invest in substantial management training programmes and link to performance management and pay;

- to use service improvement as a marketing tool;

- to keep service innovations and initiatives within a current strategic framework.

The provider will need to understand how total customer orientation is perceived, i.e. externally the provider is seen as:

- responsive to customer need;

- a good listener;

- adding value through innovative products and services;

- sharing data and taking part in joint problem solving – generally seeking a partnership approach;

- recognising the importance of third party accreditation in creating customer confidence;

- understanding the customer's business and the factors critical to their success;

- caring about the way they deal with each customer;

- enabling competitors to see the client company as formidable;

- enabling shareholders to see the client company as a safe, worthwhile investment;

- enabling communities to see the client company as a caring partner.

Finally, to ensure that future employees see the client company as one they would be proud to work for.

Internally, a great provider will have a style of operation which is characterised by service and quality being part of every routine meeting and influencing every decision. Systematic data driven approaches to problem solving involve everyone and are visibly displayed and problems are seen as opportunities, root causes are identified and once resolved the same problems rarely recur.

The vision continues: employee investment is reflected by people being valued, trust abounding and personal recognition and reward occurring naturally. Employees are proud of their work, their colleagues and their company and actively promote the virtues of the company. Training is readily available and eagerly sought by everyone for both job and personal development and everyone knows their customers and what is expected by their customers.

Management behaviour is based on visionary and overt leadership, clearly championing service quality improvement and leading by example, setting clear priorities and targets, creating a climate for continuous improvement, role modelling, improvement by learning and practising new techniques, carefully choosing improvement projects for others to be involved in, listening to staff, responding to ideas non-defensively, using coaching as a means to problem solving and eliminating blame and breaking down barriers to get problems solved rather than protecting territory, sharing information openly and not using it as a power source.

If these outsource providers live the vision that they are trying to deliver for their clients, the benefits are mutually rewarding:

- Guaranteed service quality becomes a marketable product in itself with a price differential acceptable to the customer.

- Quality improvement provides a cost effective organisation since waste, re-work and compensation become a thing of the past.

- A common purpose and alignment removes compartmentalisation and generates trust and enthusiasm.

- A better educated more numerate management and workforce are better prepared to face and handle change more confidently and without fear. Change becomes welcomed and sought after and cries for stability disappear.

- Management systems and processes are updated and the climate of continuous improvement ensures they are regularly reviewed for effectiveness, amended or removed.

- Energy and potential are released at all levels to create an altogether more powerful, innovative and responsive organisation.

- Partnership programmes ensure only the best suppliers are kept, and effort on new business generation is reduced as growth comes from customer loyalty and mutual development.

Issues arising for providers are concerned with facts that:

- Quality is personal and emotional rather than technical and therefore difficult to measure and replicate.

- Customers make judgments based on personal perceptions.

- Customers have choice.

- Enormous scope exists for creating customer loyalty and competitive edge.

- Providers must get things *consistently* right in the eyes of the customer.

- Competitive advantage must be based on a noticeable difference which meets identified customer needs rather than others.

- Service is a strategic issue and mechanisms must be put in place to make service a key organisational value.

It's worth considering as a client what are you really buying, it certainly isn't a product or service, it is more time, efficiency, peace of mind, space, expertise. What's really going on in your world?

The clients most equipped to deal with the challenges of the future will be using information and technology to respond to changing circumstances and expectations. They will realise that the competitive environment will no longer tolerate slow response or delayed decision making. Managing this process will require whole company commitment and to get this, the management communication with and the motivation of people will be the top two priorities. Employees will have to be continually exposed to and reminded of ways to develop relationships within and outside the organisation. The organisation by looking after employees in the best possible way will be a 24-hour role model of total customer centricity. The decision makers involved in the management of the Human Resources activities, whether outsourced, insourced or co-sourced, must be dedicated to preparing for the eventuality of everything.

About the author

Sally Vanson is Head of Human Resources for MCL Group Ltd, a group of 13 companies which include Mazda Cars UK Ltd, Kia Cars UK Ltd, Amethyst Group, and Autoflow Logistics. She is also a Director of Performance First Ltd and Performance Outsourcing Ltd, companies dedicated to enabling extraordinary change, development and growth in organisations through inspirational resolutions to business concerns. At MCL Group Ltd she has been responsible for setting up a state of the art HR system, including Performance Management, Competence and Capability models and an HR account management system backed up with a service level agreement. It is this model which created her interest and expertise in Outsourcing, an area in which she is gaining a reputation as an international speaker.

The author may be contacted via the publishers.

CHAPTER 1

Why outsource Human Resources?

Ask why not, not why!

The question 'What is Human Resources?' has as many answers as the number of people and organisations trying to answer it. Commonality among answers covers the following characteristics:

- The enabling of the realisation of an organisation's goals through professional management and support of the people involved.

- The integration of a company's needs and its people's needs.

- The care and welfare of people.

- The development of core competences through people.

- The growth of an organisation through its human environment.

- The maintenance of a positive and effective social climate by motivating people within a supportive culture.

- The integrated service support around strategies, structure and organisation, personnel administration, recruitment and selection, training and development, competence and capability development, compensation and benefits, industrial relations, information and communication, legislation and the management of diversity.

A more interesting question could be around the purpose of Human Resources. Having the right people in the right place at the right time with the right knowledge, skills and attitudes to serve the right customers in the right way every time is a common response. This can be backed up through the accomplishment of goals, roles and processes with a high degree of quality and productivity, within economic goals of the organisation, within a positive climate which promotes dialogue, concentration and participation and facilitates personal development, optimisation of talent and is concerned with personal satisfaction, self-esteem, identity and happiness. Or controversially, is it about paper generation and work justification for a small number of people who enjoy getting paid for turning up?

This poses a challenge indeed. How can organisations provide a totally aligned experience for themselves and their people?

Definitions of 'outsourcing'

- Breibart (*HR Planner Newsletter*, 1996, p3) suggests that outsourcing is *'the transfer of the management or administration of a process or function from in-house staff to an outside service provider'*.

- Harkins in 1996 indicates that outsourcing means *'having an external vendor provide, on a recurring basis, a service that would normally be performed within the organisation. Whilst this is a convenient shorthand definition, the concept of outsourcing clearly captures a broader range of strategic partnerships. Think of it as a continuum that contains discrete relationships with consultants on the one end, service or function providers in the middle and broader arrangements such as employee leasing, virtual organisations and webs of inclusion on the other'*.

- KPMG (1996) talk about *Business Process Outsourcing* as the *'delegation of one or more business processes to an external provider, who then owns, manages and administers the selected processes based on defined and measurable performance metrics'*.

In his book – *The Age of Unreason* – Charles Handy suggests that 'less than half of the workforce in the industrialized world will be in "proper" full-time jobs in organisations by the beginning of the twenty-first century'. He, like many others, goes on to suggest that organisations will focus on core work, that task orientated or generic work will be contracted out to those who are expert at it, that there will be a vast number of portfolio workers who have several roles or contracts with a variety of employers to whom they provide services, and that there will be a focus on getting customers to do their own work e.g. training consultants get their clients to produce their own manuals according to the specification of the consultant, who is following the client's brief.

While Handy's predication may be wide of the mark at the moment – April 2001 – there is no doubt that there is massive change in the way Human Resource functions are handled in organisations. Financial pressures are forcing Human Resources into the arms of outsourcing providers. The departments rarely get a huge slice of capital investment and at a time when the requirements of the functions are exploding in terms of headcount, space taken up in buildings, purchasing software, i.e. personnel and payroll systems and now building their own portals, outsourcing becomes an attractive option. Many Human Resources departments are being asked to do more with less, and outsourcing can alleviate the need to spend money in these areas and time on re-engineering processes.

For small and medium size companies a full time HR function can be too expensive to contemplate. The paradox is that so, of course, can getting it wrong and ending up in an employment tribunal or in conflict with the Inland Revenue. However outsourcing is not the panacea for everyone. Traditional family companies will probably need it less due to their informal operating environment. For the companies that do see it as a viable and cost effective alternative to their current arrangements, due diligence is key before any active discussions with providers take place. The future direction of the client company, the availability and size of the HR budget can determine the decision as will the current head of Human Resources issues and that person's willingness to work for the provider. Another issue to resolve is whether the client is willing and able to absorb changes into its IT structure, especially if the outsourcer is going to be using proprietary software, and whether the online capacity is available.

Many companies find it hard to part with the control of functions which involve people, either because of the emotion attached or the importance of the asset, e.g. Sales, Marketing, and Human Resources. The Human Resources department and its involvement with compliance, i.e. safety, health, life insurance, compensation and benefits, employment legislation etc. makes the prospect even more of a risk to some clients. These are critical issues and the arrangements are key because outsourcing does not reduce or redefine the employer responsibility for these areas.

Human Resources outsourcing includes:

1. Professional Employment Organisations – who lease employees to the business, pay them and take legal responsibility for them; they are in effect co-employers.

2. Business Process Outsourcing – which is the systems and intranet application of the function, generally using the latest technology and operating a self service function.

3. Applications Service Providers – who host Human Resources software that manages payroll, benefits, employee record keeping etc. on behalf of the client.

There are many derivations of these as discussed later in the book, but whichever route is chosen at the very least clients considering outsourcing solutions should review payroll, benefits administration, recruitment and compliance, conflict resolution and standard policies and procedures.

When going down the outsourcing route the client may also want to consider a menu of provision, a pilot period within a dedicated team, and would want to take up references from similar size businesses in similar industries.

For many years in the UK companies have outsourced their employee services and facilities services, e.g. security, cleaning, catering etc. Automotive manufacturers have outsourced component manufacturing and preassembly activity, logistics companies have outsourced their distribution. Small companies, not being large enough to carry the overhead have traditionally outsourced accounting and professional service work, fulfilment houses have outsourced piece work to home workers. More recently with the advent of call and contact centres, companies are outsourcing their customer assistance and customer service functions. An interesting trend due to complicated employment legislation in Europe, and high costs associated with employment has been to locate these centres overseas, notably India and other labour intensive functions, e.g. sales and bought ledger activity are following this lead. Most of these activities however have been traditionally low risk and tactical. The Benefits Agency at the Department of Social Security in the UK outsource almost every non core function. Their transition of 5,400 government workers to the private sector was seen as a pioneering activity across Europe and is a useful model for complicated multifunctional organisations to follow.

From these examples it can be seen that outsourcing happens at varying levels:

- Individual or specialist

- Functional

- Task, usually labour intensive.

So far there is little evidence of outsourcing the whole process. Within Human Resources it is more common for larger organisations to retain the strategic input and decision making activity and outsource some or all of the task (there are many combinations of this) and for smaller organisations to retain the task but to outsource the specialist areas such as HR strategy, legislative advice and sometimes pensions administration and payroll. However trends suggest that this will change quickly and that organisations will bundle many different functions together into a total package of outsourced support services that provide more integrated and coordinated solutions at reduced cost levels. This will have the added benefit of integrating other 'best in class' service providers with a single point of contact for a whole range of services.

As Human Resources becomes the latest focus of many boards as they grapple with balanced scorecard and other measures and try to quantify the value of Human Resources, it too is under the outsourcing spotlight. The evolution of technology adds to this as the quantifiable nature of these tasks allows them to be ring fenced and a focus to evolve towards the strategic activities of Human Resources.

As mentioned previously, the outsourcing of individual or specialist activities usually covers the movement of specific roles out of the organisation. This could be the payroll clerk, the recruitment specialist, the in-house trainer, often where the dependency is on one person and the function is difficult to manage in times of holiday, sickness etc. and difficult to replace immediately when a vacancy occurs. There are also management issues as the manager may not have the technical expertise to know when the individual is performing well or the competence to cover in times of emergency. Within small organisations, the budget is just not available to support the employment of these specialists, resulting in increasing propensity for small companies to subscribe to legislative help lines, on-call Human Resource management and strategists as well as specialist consultants.

At the functional level, there can be similar problems often caused by a functional team reporting to a non functional director or other functional specialist (e.g. how often do Human Resources managers still report to the Finance Director?); this means there can be a lack of support and understanding for the function, subjective decisions made about the functional effectiveness, resulting in demotivation, diminishing productivity and often defections of key employees.

Lastly at the task level, organisations are being strangled by ever increasing legislation and bureaucracy. Other commercial demands on management lead to companies losing patience and getting rid of the headache of labour intensive activity. This is not always a cost based decision, but based on the logic of co-dependent working with each partner focusing on what s/he does well.

Key social issues are changing the way that organisational Human Resources is evolving:

- The growth in service industries and decline in manufacturing gives rise to increasing affluence. This allows the employees more say in employment terms and conditions and has led to flexible and home working.

- Changes in employment structure, more women in the economy, company downsizing – stripping out layers of middle management, changing patterns of family life and marriage, a mortgage driven society and transient work forces.

- Technology, remote working, continuity of experience via sophisticated customer relationship management activity, ease of contract labour.

- Commercial competition leads to outsourcing to reduce over-head not just in financial terms, but also in terms of work/life balance and expenditure of time and stress. Management want to increase focus, to flexibly adjust to peaks and troughs and downsizing is trendy. Property ownerships and fixed work stations are expensive overheads – companies are seeing a benefit in virtual operations.

- The whole Human Resource function is perceived as a political headache. From managing employment legislation, to trying to recruit the right person with the right skills and attitude to the right job – which may change in six months' time, to pensions administration to training and development; it is often still regarded as a cost and not as an investment, difficult to evaluate and to get employees to commit to.

The frustrations of people issues at board level, the lack of a measurement matrix, the emotive perceptions of the Human Resources function, coupled with the following commercial changes are leading strategists to court outsourcing as an important factor in sustainability and survival.

Commercial change has accelerated:

- Large corporations are no longer competitive. The 20+ layers of global management are perceived as a strangulation process, and this overlaid with diverse and multi-functional task to support the core competence of the corporation is viewed as a recipe for disaster.

- Small flexible companies can change overnight. 'An internet year is three months' – the pace of change has to be instant.

- Customer centricity demands a response yesterday – this is equally true for internal customers (employees) as for externals. The functions have to be slick and aligned to business purpose.

- Stakeholders are demanding and getting focused management teams that deliver value adding results. Companies have to focus on core competences and customer centricity.

- Sustainable profitable growth depends on more than financial monitoring and reporting. The strategic health of organisations is constantly under the spotlight in the challenge to predict future profitability and therefore net worth of the company.

- Interim management and technical specialists are plentiful as those individuals focus on trends for work/life balance and no longer want a 'job for life'. Similarly others want a quality of life and to work nearer home in traditional areas of high unemployment. Outsourcing companies can reduce cost by locating response teams in areas where pay and property are cheaper.

- The technological and knowledge management revolution means that some companies can no longer attract state of the art players. This can be due to location, brand reputation, culture as well as career opportunities. An outsourcing company will allow the Human Resources specialist to achieve his/her potential in his/her chosen area of expertise as a full player in a like minded team, as opposed to being a minority player in a lower division of an industrial conglomerate.

In Human Resources itself factors are emerging:

- More Human Resources representatives are sitting on main boards than ever before, becoming strategic planning partners and setting major policy. The function is increasingly involved in strategic planning decisions.

- Human Resources must therefore have a full commercial understanding of the business.

- Advanced technology has assisted the trend for 'self-service' Human Resource activity where employees and management take over their own record keeping and manage their own computer based training and learning.

- Human Resources departments have to be cost justified and benefit evaluation is difficult especially in areas of employee assistance. Human Resources are expected to provide value adding services.

- Organisations are looking to gain competitive edge through their people. People (skills, knowledge, attitude, application and emotional intelligence) are the distinguishing fingerprints of commercial success.

- Human Resources has to communicate how it contributes and demonstrate its value to the bottom line.

- Human Resources must now be a strategic alliance with line management and involve them in the development of HR policy.

- The Human Resources framework has changed to one of competence-based, structural, and process orientated profitability.

In order to be able to focus on strategic issues, many Human Resources directors are getting partners to manage the daily task. Alan Little of PricewaterhouseCoopers suggests 'this frees up valuable management time and energy that can be better spent on strategic planning initiatives that add more value to the company, rather than programme administration with all of its complexities and many details'.

Current trends suggest that most companies that have outsourced in the past like the solution and go back for more. Ninety per cent of the current outsourcing projects that are being planned come from clients who are currently outsourcing – some of this is due to a boost from the business process outsourcing which gains ground quickly because of new and innovative technology. The outsourcing of Human Resources activities is only five years old at the time of writing and suggestions are that this is increasingly rapidly.

Aon Consulting suggest that many companies only look at the short term effects of outsourcing due to an immediate need and that they would be more effective if they looked at the long term impacts or benefits as well. Terry Terhark says that 'preparation is critical when outsourcing any portion of the staffing because it is such a big change. Outsourcing suppliers will come in with new and different models and a company needs to prepare its people for what the new process may be. They need to be very clear over who is accountable for what and how the provider will be managed and measured. This change process is doubly challenging and getting used to a new employment and a new Human Resources system is difficult for general and HR employees'. Terry Terhark recommends using a disciplined and regimented process in determining the best provider.

Potential clients need to understand the supplier market. Outsourcing companies are a growth industry. Outsourcing is a strategy for rapid growth within service organisations and Human Resources in particular is a scalable process on a global basis. Some functions, e.g. logistics, are difficult to take into different countries where different assets are involved whereas Human Resources have economies of scale. To operate effectively you do not need 20 different payroll systems and 50 different recruiters.

There are also economies of scope. Companies are often already outsourcing processes on a stand alone basis, but not the whole function which may include more than 20 individual process areas.

Exult recognised these characteristics early on as part of their start up strategy. They then added a global niche plan, i.e. Global 500 companies with more than 25,000 employees and more than $10 billion in turnover and a guarantee to take on a client's existing employees and went for it. They are justifiably proud of a management team that knows how to manage a five to ten year outsourcing contract and their world class IT expertise.

It is vital that the provider's IT and HR knowledge and application is world class. How else are they able to build web portals? An enormous amount of capital is needed both for technology and bricks and mortar, as contact centres need to be built not bought. How else can clients and systems be added to centres that were designed to support specific clients and projects?

Another key to a successful provider is an anchor client and this is usually the first large client who is prepared to be a reference site, one who is using innovative services and getting excellent results. This client will have spectacular case studies that the provider can use in marketing literature, as conference topics etc. and will be prepared to host visits from prospective buyers in return for discounted services, corporate public relations, brand alignment, and joint marketing or other value adding incentives.

Reasons for outsourcing

- Reduce costs through supplier's volume purchasing, lower cost structure and enhanced expertise.

- Fixed costs become variable costs.

- Service level agreements provide measurable cost/benefit analysis against pre defined productivity levels.

- Reduces tie up of working capital in balance sheet and enables resources to be freed up for investment, research and development.

- Improves cash flow as credit obtained through costs being invoiced by provider.

- Admin costs and headcount can be reduced.

- Reciprocal sales can be gained through portfolio marketing via supplier's network.

- Growth is easily coped with by tapping in to supplier's expertise, systems and more enhanced capability.

- Temporary expansion can be dealt with by amendment to contract without long term liability. This allows the organisation increased flexibility and rapid response times.

- Company can focus on and exploit core skills.

- Employees in outsourced function have a greater potential career path, therefore, personal development and commitment are enhanced.

- This results in increased energy and commerciality in non-core areas.

- Operating performance and quality is improved.

- Access to skills and capability, which may not have been available.

- More professional and credible Human Resource function, which is seen as an external service rather than internal support.

- Improved risk management, with appropriate decision making time allocated to the function.

- Opportunity to gain creativity and innovation.

- Organisational change and transformation easily managed.

- Both partners focus on what they do best.

- Employees feel valued through perception of external care.

- Added value to all stakeholders.

An overall strategy

To understand the full benefit the organisation needs to ask if the decision to outsource is a short-term operational function viewpoint or if it is part of a larger business process re-engineering strategy. It is in terms of the latter that a complete process review and the full power and added value can be seen.

The company needs to consider the long-term strategic impact. Areas to include:

1. The future vision and mission.

2. The shape of the organisation.

3. Competence and capability demanded in the future.

4. Impact of loss of skill and knowledge to outsource provider.

5. The history and knowledge management issue.

6. Loss of competitive advantage.

7. Impact on culture, branding, beliefs and values. The psychological contract.

8. Future flexibility and performance.

9. Change to financial structure and balance sheet.

All these areas are interrelated and aligned, as one considers the trend from the large functional silos and vertical integration of the past, and the new shapes of customer centric, process driven, team based working, e.g. the dot.coms. Thus the vision from the very top must be firmly established along the lines of the McKinsey 7 's' model in order for the strategy to be objective.

Inclusiveness and integration are stressed throughout this book. This must happen through and between each of the seven values. Total alignment with the corporate vision and mission is key to success.

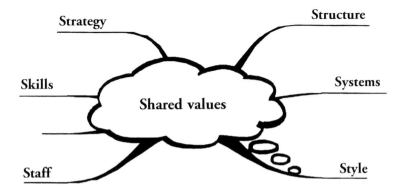

Figure 1 Developing a shared vision.

There may also be a pressure to keep Human Resources activities in house. Where people are highly valued in an organisation and where there is support from the chief executive officer in particular, Human Resources can be viewed as a core activity. Those who really prize knowledge and talent as a unique selling point will be careful as to what is kept and what is outsourced. In a unionised environment there is concern over how a supplier would cope with industrial action and where their loyalties would lie. The service level agreement and the psychological contract are key.

Questions to consider:

1. What issues are up for resolution?

2. What specific evidence is there that these are facts?

3. What are the symptoms of these problems?

4. What would happen if the situation were left as it is?

5. Who stands to gain by the change?

6. Which other functions are being outsourced?

7. What other options are there to resolve the issues?

8. Why was outsourcing chosen?

9. How will this impact on other internal processes?

10. Who is on the project team?

11. How were they chosen?

12. What value will each person add?

13. How will each person limit the decision making effectiveness?

14. Who are the 'worms and diamonds'?

15. What measurable results will be achieved?

16. What are the key success factors?

17. What are the barriers to success?

18. What will be the impact of failure?

A basic tool to resolve some of the questions around 'to outsource or not to outsource' is the S.C.O.R.E. model. This involves making a causal loop of the 'problem space'. Questions to ask about each element of the process are:

- What is the **symptom** in this problem?

- What is the **cause** of the symptom in this problem?

- What is the desired **outcome** or goal relating to this problem?

- What would be the longer term **effect** of reaching this goal?

- What **resource** would help address the cause?

- What **resource** would help achieve the outcome?

It is then possible to chunk down into the deep structures behind the causal loops identified. These deep structures will relate to the interactions between the systems. According to work done in systemic Neuro Linguistic Programming there are three fundamental system deep structures:

- Balancing

- Escalating

- Optimising

Balancing questions therefore will address those areas which need to work in harmony while address variable issues, e.g. a balance between investment and expenditure – will the outsource activity require any up front investment or expenditure and how will that sit with a strategic objective about cost reduction or return on investment?

Escalating questions will support processes, which encourage deviation or difference. For example, a company that wants to grow may want to increase market penetration. There may be added value in an outsourcing alliance with regard to reciprocal selling, i.e. the opportunity to sell into the other customers of the outsourcing provider, while recommending the outsourcing provider to current customers of the client company. This would involve finding the resources necessary to achieve the meta or higher level outcome by identifying and removing obstacles to progress, e.g. ignorance, misunderstanding of need, fear of new ways of working and perception of loss of control. These are very different from balancing issues where constant monitoring is required to reach harmony between two elements. In an escalating system there is no attempt to reach balance, rather a goal to remove obstruction. The timeframes are different as well. In balancing there is an ongoing, continuous process and escalation efforts typically run in short bursts.

Optimising questions are a combination of balance and escalation. This is about reducing some elements and variations while encouraging and maximising others. A good example of this is an attempt to reach total quality, e.g. to escalate the condition of quality of service, while simultaneously reducing rate of defects. This could be represented by a 'tug of war' and requires continuous vigilance to maintain the total quality state. It is this area that is the goal for effective outsourcing relationships and the challenge is to reframe the 'tug of war' mentality of old school contracted out services, e.g. the stereotypical works canteen type of activity, into a partnership alliance that is mutually supportive in a quest for excellence.

Once the vision is understood the decision makers will understand the need for change, the need to focus on core competences to meet customer need and how 'doing what we've always done will result in what we've always had'.

Outsourcing will then assist in being a catalyst for change and unfreeze some of the old constraints, thus supporting a strategy of enhanced flexibility around a central focus on customers. Instead of employees being part of some remote administrative support function (they have been called 'non-productives' or 'non-professionals', in some famous organisations) every direct employee can understand how they add value to the customer. (This will include those employees now employed by the outsource supplier as their previous colleagues become their customers.)

When outsourcing becomes such a strategic initiative and results in a complete restructure, it becomes a visible and significant sign to all employees that the organisation is very serious about the change and usually mobilises the workforce to get behind the new world or admit they can't cope and move on. It allows the management of the Human Resources function to become a top down, project driven activity with less risk than the internal management due to measurable service level agreements and objective, professional and credible client reviews.

In 1998 the Global Top Decision Makers Study on Business Process Outsourcing, sponsored by PricewaterhouseCoopers and conducted by Yankleovich Partners, interviewed top executives at 304 of the world's largest companies in 14 countries. These senior executives reported their findings from outsourcing:

- 91% greater administrative efficiency;

- 86% more time to focus on core business;

- 85% increased shareholder value;

- 81% improved service quality;

- 76% helping with competitive advantage;

- 64% assistance in meeting changing customer demands.

A decision to improve performance

Where the decision to outsource is made in isolation, this can be due to the Human Resources department having become slow and cumbersome, especially in organisations with stable profitability and long serving employees. The decision then becomes more of a 'spring clean' of the comfort zone, a gaining of objectivity, often with cost reduction attached as overhead can increase over the years with familiarity. Often the internal team will be forced to bid alongside external tenders (generally in the public sector) and the process will force an objective review of the function alongside informed market research. A key question to ask is around how they would perform differently and add value under a new contract?

Another argument for outsourcing Human Resources is that it is not an area where a company needs to spend a large amount of resource. This says a lot about the company's value systems and beliefs in the contribution of people to the bottom line. It may well vary by industry and often between direct and indirect service providers and manufacturers.

Another reason for changing is to reduce headcount, and this result will almost always happen, but will often generate paper savings rather than true reductions in payroll cost. This is because the non-headcount workers will often be the same employees, transferred from the client, and with the providers' costs and sometimes salary increases added back in.

A creative option

To minimise risk some companies decide to re-insource the out-source function. This is about moving the tasks and responsibilities elsewhere within the organisation, i.e. set up their own subsidiary to run the Human Resources function and sell the products and services to other organisations thus recouping their own investment in the resource, retaining control and minimising risk in the future with the added benefit of a diversified profit centre. They even gain buy-in and commitment from the employees through equity options. This allows the organisation to retain some control and have the benefits of outsourcing. Service level agreements can still be set up, and contribution can be gained through an external customer base of selling the services to third parties.

....

Case study

Performance First Ltd is an example of being creative. MCL Group was working in partnership with Performance First, jointly designing and delivering successful development programmes for their employees. Performance First needed premises, administrative support etc and MCL need financial contribution to the Human Resources function in order to carry on with state of the art development during difficult trading conditions. A strategic alliance was formed whereby Performance First became based in a MCL building with administrative support in return for 25% of its profit and discounted training and development solutions for MCL. The WIN:WIN results allowed a small business to reduce liabilities through variable overhead and a larger organisation to gain contribution to what was perceived as an overhead cost while maintaining and developing the service offering to their employees.

....

One different way of viewing insourcing is that of stopping the Human Resources function doing some work rather than encouraging others to do it. This often happens where the HR function has become too strong and influential and for political reasons, usually through fear, Boards decide to downsize it through restructure. The concern with this is that root cause has not been discussed for the decision and that where others are assigned the work, e.g. payroll to finance or treasury departments, these people are rarely given the time, the training and development to carry out the new tasks. And the relationship that would have allowed coaching and mentoring from the previous 'expert' group has been broken.

A word of warning here as there are some predications that as costs mount Human Resources will eventually retake control of its previous tasks and responsibilities, however this could be wisdom with hindsight, i.e. all the benefits of learning through the process can be reapplied internally and after all, the business world does go round in cycles.

An often forgotten question is that of deciding the best time to outsource. Like looking for new employment, the best time is often not when demotivated with the current proposition. Rather like other life changing decisions this should be approached from a position of strength and be demand led. A good time could be during expansion, when the organisation is looking for world class performance, needs to improve or grow capability, loses key players and therefore needs to boost internal competence, and when the longer term business strategy will support short term upheaval.

CHAPTER 2

What to include and what to retain

'Aligning people towards the future
not cementing them
in the past.'

A valuable resource in developing understanding about which elements of Human Resources to outsource is the Department of Trade and Industry's (DTI) research on sustaining success through people.

Five paths to sustained success

Some broad bands of management practice, which companies researched by the DTI project have identified as producing a balanced environment in which employees thrived and sought success for themselves and their organisations:

- Shared goals – understanding the business we are in.

- Shared culture – agreed values which bind us together.

- Shared learning – continuously improving ourselves.

- Shared effort – one business driven by flexible teams.

- Shared information – effective communication throughout the company.

These provide key business benefits.

Shared goals

- plans pull people together – providing a shared direction;

- shared planning enables employees to see how they fit in to the organisation and the contribution they are making;

- senior management receive ideas from those who really understand the problems,

- and the opportunities.

Shared culture

- all employees feel respected and so give of their best;

- employees are confident and optimistic – they feel they are 'winners'.

- the culture supports the organisation's competitive strategy and provides the energy to sustain it, stretching and extending both the company and the individual.

Shared learning

- the company realises a high return from its commitment to its people;

- there is a constant stream of improvements within the company;

- the entire organisation becomes increasingly receptive to change;

- individuals get increased job satisfaction from their new skills;

- career and personal development plans increase loyalty.

Shared effort

- people work better when they feel they are part of a group;

- teams can achieve more than a collection of individuals;

- essential co-operation across the whole organisation is maintained.

Shared information

- employees have the information needed to set objectives and priorities;

- senior managers know what is actually going on;

- the company reacts rapidly to threats and opportunities;

- trust and respect are reinforced throughout the company.

Some core questions to ask would be around:

- How to define, promote, gain consistent involvement and buy-in.

- Sustaining behaviours that underpin the values.

- Recruiting and developing against brand values.

These would then develop into issues around the challenge of managing the performance of the clients' and the third party employees.

The decision maker will have to take into account the generic Human Resources objectives, which apply to all businesses, namely:

- To provide a qualitative and cost effective Human Resources function to support the company in maximising contribution of people to bottom-line.

- To enable the company to comply with legislation through well researched and up to date Human Resources policies and procedures implemented and monitored with minimum bureaucracy and paperwork.

In all of this understanding the Human Resources strategy is core. Strategy is about the deployment of the available resources to achieve the business success. These resources will include the

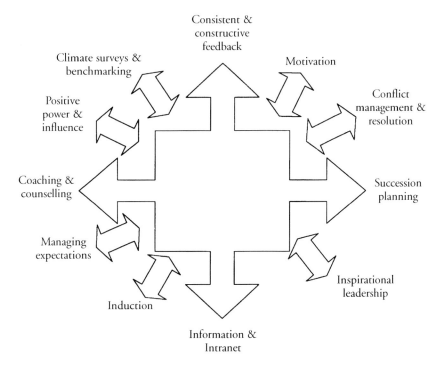

Consistent &
constructive
feedback

Climate surveys &
benchmarking

Motivation

Positive
power &
influence

Conflict
management &
resolution

Coaching &
counselling

Succession
planning

Managing
expectations

Inspirational
leadership

Induction

Information &
Intranet

Figure 2 The impact of performance on HR stakeholders.

people, their time, facilities, equipment, materials, information and energy and therefore these become the components for consideration when defining what to outsource.

Fundamental questions around these elements will effect competitive advantage, the ability to develop new opportunities and anticipate future developments while avoiding surprises. Planning is key. The great client will be reviewing each element of outsourcing provision in terms of understanding the environment, the competition, resources available and using this information to identify options, make choices, decide actions and implement the decisions.

Research from Price Waterhouse in 1992 suggested that success depends on a few things being done well, questioning the unquestioned assumptions, avoid restriction to sequential logical thinking and understanding that strategic management is an ongoing process not an annual event.

Table 1 Positioning the outsourced services

Necessary evil	Customer centric	Inspirational
Efficient	Product focused	Pioneering
Maintenance	Client focused	Creative
Amateur	Competitive	Winner
Participant	Strong	Dominant
Avoidance	Risk profile	Courageous
Ignored	Industry reputation	Admired
Follower	Builds on other's ideas	Leader
Monopoly	Client structured	New entrant
Low energy	Aggressive	Brutal
Plodding	Client powered	Demanding
Undersupply	Supply/Demand	Overcapacity

The Human Resources function itself will need some analysis before decisions are taken regarding the components to outsource. The key question to ask is about the function it actually performs in the organisation. What are the outputs around advice, service, information, new knowledge and dealing with the future chaos and complexity? Is the function consultative, enabling or a service provider?

Questions to consider regarding the profile of Human Resources

- What internal image and profile is being sought?

- Who are the internal customers?

- What products and services do they need from Human Resources?

- What products and services can be provided?

- How should Human Resources be perceived?

- What is the internal perception regarding overhead cost or investment?

- What would internal customers like more of and what would they be prepared to pay?

- Where would they like the services supplied from?

- How will future Human Resources products and services be promoted?

- What financial reports are expected?

The combination of insourced and outsourced services needs to give an aligned and integrated image of being hard working and cost effective, understanding the business, professional, commercial, with integrity and rapid response times. Having said this, when outsourcing is a new concept within the client organisation it does give the opportunity to change or re-badge the Human Resources image, gain a strategic focus, encourage line management ownership, become policy advisors and enablers and move towards value adding internal consulting skills.

So what can we outsource?

- Medical and life insurance

- Manpower planning

- Recruitment (permanent, temporary and contract)

- Employee leasing

- Psychometric testing and assessment centres

- Relocation

- Training and development

- Succession planning and organisational development

- Outplacement and employee assistance programmes

- Coaching and counselling

- Compensation and benefits administration (pension and payroll)

- Record keeping and administration

- Expatriate services

One of the key issues is to ensure the supplier has more competence or adds value in a more effective way than the current in house employees.

Medical and life insurance

Most companies will outsource their medical and life insurance to avoid the risk of large losses. Self insurance can seem cheaper in the short term but a few large claims could bankrupt the fund. Many medical insurance suppliers throw in life insurance and for large numbers of employees there is very little paperwork involved.

Self insurance involves increased headcount in terms of administration, enquiry handling and specialist knowledge in the UK to deal with vast amounts of legislation around compliance.

Pricing is an issue for smaller companies who have no advantages from which to negotiate on rate. The result can be a grouping together to share purchasing power, e.g. Best Western Marketing Consortium, Federation of Small Businesses and the new online communities such as Motivano.

Large companies can negotiate often to minimal pricing levels, and for these annual reviews and going through a tender process is key to maintaining an edge. Once these companies take over the management of these services, they get basic data about employees from the employer. Their role is then to maintain eligibility records, translate the information into what plans they are eligible for, send the appropriate information and cost of plan to the employee and once accepted, enrol them with the provider. They then liaise with the payroll provider over deductions. This enables employees to change status direct once they change domestic circumstances and the employer to get regular management information re claims etc.

Success is derived from a partnership arrangement with both sides having continuous and open dialogue about current and new issues, initiating new processes, use of Intranet and expanding the service provision.

Technology is the biggest enabler to outsourcing employee benefits. Some outsource suppliers, e.g. Motivano, will operate a complete web based benefits management programme, with varying levels of access and package to look after a variety of employee needs. This packaged service covers pensions, medical cover, dental and optical cover, insurance as well as employee perks and communication tools (discussed elsewhere).

Manpower planning

This is about ensuring the organisation has the right people with the right skills, knowledge and attitude, in the right place at the right time. Manpower planning drops straight out of the Human Resources strategy into the Human Resources planning process. If it is outsourced it is usually on a consultancy or retainer basis, and happens periodically after the business planning process or at times of merger, acquisition or organic growth of the business.

There are five basic steps:

1. Reviewing the future plans of the client company, and this could be from either a growth, stability or downsizing perspective.

2. Carrying out an audit of existing labour force against defined future need. This can be by numbers, location, skills, working hours and preferences or any other categorisation decided by the client.

3. Identify possible movement of employees. This could be due to retirement, relocation, maternity issues, disabilities, long term sickness, customer or project losses, redundancy, unsuitability for retraining, TUPE, etc.

4. Forecast short, medium and long term scenarios. These are based on business requirements, availability and suitability of current personnel, workload, customer requirements, economic forecasts, evolving skills levels etc.

5. Developing an action plan with timescales, key success factors, over short, medium and long-term periods with review dates and costings.

Much information is required to complete manpower planning and will involve a close relationship with the personnel systems provider and conversations with line managers.

Recruitment

Recruitment is the process of attracting applicants to the job so the client company can choose the most appropriate candidate. It goes hand in hand with selection procedures in the current climate, and these will vary from brief interviews to full blown assessment centres. Whatever happens the process should result in attracting the most appropriate applicants and discouraging time wasters. Outsourced recruitment is lucrative and can consume huge amounts of time and resource while being an enormous challenge to the management processes.

With changing employment practices, new legislation and heightened competition in the labour market, the ways in which employees are recruited and selected can have massive short and long term effects on company performance. Leading companies are already making recruitment strategy an HR priority and studies show that the cost of recruitment errors is greater than the cost of implementing an effective strategy.

Outsourcing of recruitment can involve all or part of the spectrum from:

- consulting with line management on needs, role profile, person specification, market rate, incentive packages etc;

- provision of permanent, temporary and contract labour;

- labour market assessment;

- dealing with media from writing and placing of advertisements, space purchase and billing;

- executive, specialist search activities;

- post box activity, telephone interviewing, accepting, screening and short listing of applicants;

- initial in depth interviews, testing and assessment centres;

- management/joint interviewing of final applicants with line managers;

- reference checking, and

- new employee follow-ups once in post.

According to Watson Wyatt, by showing a significant improvement in recruiting new talent, companies can achieve a 10.1% increase in market value – added value through shareholder benefit.

When outsourcing recruitment, the organisation needs to have an understanding of the overall entry process, the importance of feedback, analysis and clear communication and to check the understanding of recruitment techniques and selection methods and their alignment with the culture, not to mention clearly defined responsibilities in terms of understanding and applying employment legislation. For example, in an 'e' commerce environment there is a need to check out personal and business skills and the ability to apply these as well as technical know-how. The recruitment process has to be fast, flexible and friendly to attract key players and get them on board before competitors. Of course a major benefit of outsourcing recruitment is that the supplier is only paid once the candidate is employed. (This will differ with retainer fees paid upfront for executive search.)

European employers are agreeing that job dedication and company loyalty are no longer the pre-requisites in job seekers. Strong communication skills and a willingness to adapt to change are key and this must be reflected in the employment process. Many companies find themselves lagging in the race to keep up with X-ray like recruitment techniques, distrusting or fearing the techno phobia, and the stress caused when line managers chase the HR department is one good reason to let the experts resolve the problem.

Legislation affecting recruitment

- The Fairness at Work White Paper.

- Employment Relations Act 1999.

- Equal Pay Act 1970/Equal Pay (Amendment Act) 1983.

- Sex Discrimination Act 1975/Sex Discrimination (Amendment) Act 1986.

- Race Relations Act 1976.

- Disability Discrimination Act 1995/Disability Discrimination (Amendment) Act 1997.

- Age diversity in employment.

- The Pensions Act 1995.

- The Welfare Reform and Pensions Bill 1999.

Increasingly recruitment activity is being partially outsourced to the online recruiters. Despite predictions that this would not work, job applications that once took weeks can be processed in minutes. An estimated 31% of web users in the UK have looked for a job online and 61% suggest they would use the Internet to find their next job. Traditional recruitment firms now have a presence on the Internet as well as their bricks and mortar sites. The explosion of suppliers in this area is causing confusion and the battle for market share varies from huge multinationals to small local providers.

The big five firms of consultants are employing varying competitive strategies from expensive marketing campaigns, mergers and acquisitions, strategic partnership and now the development of software solutions. They gain their revenue by charging separately for advertising and for assessment.

Online recruitment also saves time and cost. Some companies choose to establish their own online recruitment agency, supported through a third party agency. For example, a line manager can now post a vacancy direct on the website and then see for themselves who is applying. Global companies will use this as a retention tool, advertising all internal vacancies and thus protecting their investment even if the employee moves to another company. Here the outsourcing activity becomes more interesting and can encompass website design and maintenance, interview and short listing activity or the whole recruitment function. Further information can be found through *Online Recruitment* magazine and job sites such as *Monster, Stepstone*, and *Top jobs on the net*. These providers themselves are unable to agree on their roles and describe themselves as online recruiters, job portals, careers portals, e-recruiters, job boards and job agencies.

The providers claim to hold large numbers of candidates, but their information varies from contact details, full CVs, completed profiles, to those who have been fully interviewed and checked out. More often than not their candidate lists are global and on completion of a skills search for a PA in Leicester, the best candidate could be in Sydney, Australia.

Concerns about bad practice, lack of confidentiality, fake jobs etc. to boost traffic numbers have led to the Recruitment and Employment Federation launching the Association of Online Recruiters to set some professional standards. They will review opportunities for information sharing, updating technological developments and lobby for policy and legislation that is practical and relevant. They are currently working with 300 known online recruiters in the UK alone, and this is difficult to track as new providers start up every day. When it comes to benchmarking, standards are not available and confusion results as potential clients are unsure as to who is actually performing versus who has the best PR and communications programme. Websites talk about numbers of hits rather than numbers of placements.

Some providers will spend huge amounts of money on publicity campaigns and for example *Monster* are happy with this strategy which supports their focus of attracting a high number of jobseekers and working with direct clients. Although the Association of Online Recruiters is currently only representing UK operators, they are hoping a European organisation will set up as the market matures and rationalises, stabilising the number of operators through mergers and acquisitions.

Monster also believe in brand building and their theme runs through their advertising to the dècor of their London offices generating an informal, dynamic and innovative approach which supports their strap line of 'work hard: relax hard'. They also believe that too much reliance on and investment in software could be an expensive mistake. *Stepstone* argue the other perspective. They have set up in every European country and promote themselves as the largest on line careers portal. *Stepstone* believe their business is growing more and more towards software and is heading the way with interactive CV analysis, intranet management and assessment tools. *Jobline* is different again with a focus on clients' retention problems, it has developed a career management system. *Jobpilot* also believe in the software investment route and has acquired a developer of web based Human Resources solutions to provide added value through salary surveys, workflow management and providing Wap functions for the jobseekers.

The prospective client will need to check the right provision for their organisation. A key aspect will be reliability and there is a need to keep an eye on the financial press. These big players have a never ending need for cash injection, and financial success will be a good indicator of how well they are performing in terms of placements.

The use of these Internet sites however increased by 100% in 2000. There are now more than 40,000 employment related websites and *Monster* has boards for 13 countries with half a million job vacancies listed. There is an enormous amount of duplication with jobs appearing on multiple sites. The downside to this is the amount of load, effort and general information 'churn'.

The client needs to be aware of the deluge of CVs that can result from these sites and this is again where the short list outsource service can step in to filter the applicants. It is currently illegal for a computer rather than a human being to draw up a shortlist (diversity would not be managed). Companies who focus on developing electronic Human Resources solutions may well have a harder ride than those like *Monster* who invest in brand building. The danger with developing generic software packages and selling them in is the real value in terms of applicability to the client business. It is important for such tools to be developed in conjunction with HR managers who know what their future employees need to be like and how they will progress through the company.

These sites, once sorted, will have increasing value as they get focused and concentrate on specific sectors, industries and/or employers. It is anticipated that some sites will start an executive search category and already on line video clips and even video interviews are becoming available. There is also a suggestion that the sophisticated sites will become forums for like minded people to network and share knowledge, developing professional communities where employers go to search for their new stars.

The success of these on line recruiters in America may not be reflected in Europe where language and geographic boundaries play a key role in mobility of the job market. Research also shows that in the UK the main reason for scanning the job sites is to get a new job, while in Germany it was to find out what was going on in the market, checking salary levels etc. and job seeking was only the fourth reason. Useage patterns therefore need to be determined on a national basis.

Employee leasing

Employers make long-term commitments when recruiting employees. This included paying them regardless of workload and when the work peaks there are not enough people, or conversely in trough periods having a fixed employee overhead can be financially crippling. By anticipating work volumes and seasonal needs, employers can opt for flexible working and maximise productivity. Capable employees who are not looking for long term assignments, who enjoy freedom and flexibility to pursue other life balancing activities, are often among the most talented and motivated.

Employee leasing has been far more applicable in the US than in the UK where there is rapid growth mainly due to employment legislation and the IR35 rules. However care needs to be taken when agreeing contracts as to the current applicability of legislation. The question of control is going to be difficult for the employer to win. An employee working on the client's premises will have to follow the client's rules and regulations and cannot make up his/her own. The leasing company is the payroll master. When leased or temporary employees are sick they are most likely to let the client know first, similarly with holiday bookings etc., although the actual financial remuneration will be agreed with the hiring company. The legislation blurs the boundaries and there is a real risk that leased or temporary employees become indistinguishable from permanent workers. A benefit of this route however is that the employing company often has additional expertise in terms of managing people and projects using the latest technology. They can also give specific training to provide expertise into companies, e.g. the two peaks in the year when the Inland Revenue need people to manage the self assessment form processing. Collating surveys and census material are other skills needed on an ad hoc basis.

Employees who are ready to learn new skills quickly and effectively can gain job security through working for an employee leasing organisation, creating career continuity and negotiating non working periods to enjoy hobbies etc. Some leasing companies will also provide generous benefits between assignments including further training and development.

Small companies find it an easy option rather than grapple with the myriad of employment issues and often the brokering fee for them is more cost effective than paying top rate for benefits and incentives because of their limited purchasing power. Another advantage therefore is that small companies can attract a better calibre of employee through levelling the benefits available between them and larger organisations.

European employment legislation is exploding. Employers must take up to date legal advice before entering into these contracts and a long term cost benefit analysis is key. A key issue with employee leasing is where the legal accountability for the employee rests and for this reason all contracts should be reviewed by employment law specialists. In some cases third party employees are deemed to be employees of the organisation actually providing the work. Similarly insurance details and negligence clauses should be carefully investigated as should the responsibility for sick pay, maternity pay etc. The EU legislation that entitles employees on fixed term contracts the same entitlements as permanent staff can be a nightmare. This will make it illegal for companies to treat fixed term staff less favourably than their permanent colleagues. Currently under consultation this legislation is taking into account whether both types of contract should be matched item by item, or by the value of the whole package. Both create administrative burdens both in terms of the initial checking and benchmarking and then ensuring they stay consistent. Some of this will be restricted by the need to find a comparator who must be in similar work and on an indefinite contract with the same employer. The DTI estimates that only half of the 1.2 million people employed in the UK on fixed term contracts work alongside similar employees on open ended contracts. Pay and pensions cannot be covered for legal reasons. The most important part of the directive is likely to be its requirement for member states to limit the use of successive fixed term contracts but collective or workplace agreements may allow this rule to vary by employer. (In the case of the leasing company, who is the employer?)

The cost bites on the realisation that fixed term employees can no longer waive their right to claim unfair dismissal at the end of their contract and that the Government is also suggesting they be included in redundancy payment schemes. Although only 5% of employees in the UK are on fixed term schemes, this rises to 12% average across Europe with up to 33% in Spain.

The reform of the employment agencies legislation in the UK could also affect employee leasing. There have been pleas for long term outsourced employees to be given exemption or special treatment in relation to quarantine periods and transfer fees. The DTI proposes that agencies will not be able to enforce a transfer fee when a temporary or leased worker takes up employment with an employer within eight weeks of the leasing contract expiring. Employers suggest that a 13 week cap would protect both parties and that the eight week cap fails to recognise the investment made by lease providers to deliver the standards of service required both by job seekers and clients. Unless repeat business can be protected many of the leasing providers will struggle to survive. The DTI argument is that these modifications would strengthen rather than inhibit market flexibility and competition and that it is not acceptable for skilled people to encounter difficulties getting permanent work with a company where they had previously been contracted.

Employee leasing can affect cash flow, as often the provider will request prepayment of one month in advance for payroll costs to enable him to pay his people on time. This should be taken into account as with permanent employees, pay is generally one month in arrears. A credit check would be a good idea to protect financial interests.

Another recent innovation in the outsourcing of recruitment is the use of global employment companies. These can be completely outsourced or can be a separate company owned and operated by the employer. Their role is to employ the workforce and then lease them out to those subsidiaries and divisions that have a requirement for their services in return for a management fee. The management fee is then used to pay the salaries, benefits and administration costs of those companies. The two major benefits are around protection for a group of high flying global employees, or streamlining a varied expatriate work population and anything in between. The main benefit is to create an international pool of employees who can be relocated anywhere. Processes and procedures are standardised to provide an efficient system.

Relocation

Relocation of employees at company expense is becoming more complicated in these days of dual income families, high property prices, long and stressful working hours, competition for labour and a 'start now' mentality.

Employers need to have a carefully thought through and costed policy which is fair and equal, adds value to the recruitment/

promotion process and is competitive. The policy should also fit the culture and values of the organisation.

What is covered under relocation?

- House hunting, travel, subsistence, use of a finders agency, paid time off for employee and partner.

- Temporary living expenses, e.g. staying in hotel, travel to work petrol, temporary property rental.

- Costs incurred in selling original property and purchasing new one, e.g. agents fees, stamp duty, capital gains tax, solicitors' fees.

- Cost of fixtures and fittings, curtains and carpets, new kitchen etc.

- Cost of moving household goods, packing and packaging, storage, service and installation, shipping of cars, boats etc.

- Finding schools, payment of loss of school fees.

- Moving and lodging domestic pets – be aware of horses and livery fees.

- Inland Revenue regulations re taxation and paying tax on tax.

Outsourcing of relocation needs to be covered by a detailed contract or service level agreement, stating pre-costed scenarios. These should include specific services, open book accounting, understanding of responsibilities regarding insurance, negligence and damage, elimination of anomalies and regular comprehensive status reports detailing progress to date of each faction with financial data, timing and next steps clearly itemised. Other areas to investigate include the relationships between the broker and sub-contractors.

The emotion involved in managing personal relocation can be empathically managed by leaving it to the experts rather than a harassed internal team, however the overall contract must be regularly monitored and reviewed. There are generally only two desired outcomes; to get the new employee productive, up and running as soon as possible and to do this within the optimum cost structure.

A complication can be the other working partner and in global companies the relocation plan needs to be fully integrated with the recruitment activity so that (policy permitting) the affectionately named 'trailing spouse' can be recruited into a suitable and local role to facilitate the transition, or introduced to alliances who may have appropriate offerings.

Training and development

Some of the biggest changes in Human Resources are taking place in training and development as the area evolves from vocational and qualification led initiatives, through the minefield of Tecs, Lecs, NVS, IIP, TDLB, and other government led acronyms to something that is becoming a living, breathing and holistic method of growing human beings. The more that behavioural issues impact on business success, the more crucial the area becomes not only to survival but grasping competitive edge. The ethos behind this is the development of high performance teams with a co-owned focus on taking their corporation to greater heights. Coaching, team and personal development and leadership are the key areas for consideration. Spiritual and emotional intelligence underpin them, add in new information and communication technology and these new working practices will have a noticeable motivational effect as well as impact on business performance.

Integrated and holistic development plans need specialist care and attention. No one person can hold the knowledge required. The use of the Internet is growing rapidly and the new economy calls for skills relating to problem solving and communication, neither of which can be taught by formal methods.

Training and development is already outsourced by most companies due to the high fixed costs of maintaining in-house and often non-specialist staff and the cost of keeping these people up to date both with state of the art training input and also internal corporate strategy, policies and process. Some companies will outsource to one provider who acts as a broker and sub contracts, others will use a variety of suppliers but the advantages of this need to be offset against the administrative requirements involved in selection, monitoring and control.

One area of interest is that of copyright. Where a training company has been contracted in to design specific course materials, then the course should be copyrighted by the company to verify ownership, unless shared ownership is agreed with the supplier. Options around this would include, a reduced fee for non-exclusive design, a royalty payment for use elsewhere, or copyrighting by the supplier in return for free use of the materials by the company. The decision should be written into the contract.

Where most training requirements are generic it makes sense to use suppliers with ready developed materials and trainers who are flexible in terms of timing and location. Key issues to question will be around:

- Need for company specialist knowledge and up to date information.

- Need for understanding of organisational strategy and implementation.

- Bespoke versus generic programmes.

- Costs of subsistence, venue hire, resources and manuals. There is an emerging trend for trainers to travel first or business class, especially when flying. The cost of this needs to be quantified against longer travel time and additional subsistence, physical stamina of trainer, current travel issues especially in UK or long haul flights. For example, at the time of writing a trainer flying Los Angeles to London was charging $5,500 business class against $985 economy.

- External accreditation and certification.

- Quality processes.

- Embedding processes, evaluation and feedback loops.

- Availability and immediacy.

- Planning cycles.

- Who will do pre and post course administration and record keeping?

An interesting example here is of Mazda Cars (UK) Ltd who retained authority, strategy and decision making in house for their dealer training, and their specialist product and technical training, but outsourced to Performance Outsourcing Ltd the supplier management, course monitoring and control, course administration, venue booking and record keeping, dealer communications, evaluation and feedback. Thus for an annual management fee, the in-house activity carried on with a headcount saving of 40% and so resulted in cost savings and a focus which when managed internally had not been possible due to employees getting involved in other functional areas or in company processes which slowed down their response times.

Another major new innovation is the advent of the company Intranet. At the BBC, employees can access details of in-company and external training programmes, arrange bookings etc. The outsource providers keep the programmes up to date because take up has a direct impact on their productivity.

From Penny Ferguson of Penny Ferguson Ltd (specialists in personal leadership programmes)

....

The times they are a changing – is training staying ahead of the game?

Is training keeping up with the speed of change happening in the business world right now? The role of the Manager has changed and will continue to change significantly – in some instances so fast that keeping up with the new ideas for effective leadership and getting the very best from our team is becoming more and more challenging.

In the old days it was fairly straight forward – you got a job, did well and were promoted. If you were lucky, you were given some skills-based management training, and continued to progress through the organisation. Many people expected to stay within the same company for their entire life, progressing up the organisation as time went by. Some companies did recognise the value of good training giving the benefit of many different workshops to develop all the required areas – presentation, motivation, leadership, change management, time management etc. To some degree, a number of the programmes available were really effective and occasionally participants retained more than the recognised 20% eight weeks later. Additionally, some actually adopted the skills as a way of life.

Bit by bit the entire working environment began to change – no longer was there job security, technology was increasingly replacing people and, at the same time, individuals were being asked to deliver more and more in less and less time. For many people their work/life balance became a joke and stress levels rocketed as they worried about how to keep up with never ending changes whilst still contributing at a level which meant they could hold on to their job. Today, this is the scenario faced by a significant percentage of managers.

The pace of change is continually increasing as new products are replaced with frightening speed. This is not going to stop – as more and more people begin working from home, virtual teams will become the norm and flexible working hours will become common. The skills required to manage the workforce of tomorrow need a very different approach and way of leading.

So what is the impact for training? Are training ideas advancing ahead of the changing business environment to enable individuals to experience the support and development that they urgently need? How, in fact, do we need to change our attitudes to training to bring it more in line with today's requirements?

I believe there is an urgent need to develop people more quickly and effectively by changing our approach to training – by taking the focus from skills training to a focus on an inside out approach. For example, we can look at skills as a tool kit that we can give to people to enable them to do the job – something that they can pick up and use dependent upon the circumstance and as required.

However, what I feel is not addressed is the need for the person to make a fundamental shift in the way that they think, the way that they view the world and the opportunity that they have to take a different level of responsibility. In working with many managers, some of the challenges I have heard recounted are things like: 'my boss won't listen to my ideas', 'the communication in our company is terrible', 'I can't do my job properly at the moment because I am waiting to hear if I am going to be made redundant', 'I haven't been given a clear job description', and so on. These statements clearly indicate that individuals feel that they are unable to have influence over their situation and have no control over dealing with these issues.

By demonstrating to these managers that in every situation and in each moment of their life they have 100% responsibility available to them and then asking how much responsibility they feel they are taking right now I usually find that the reality is they are only taking about 30-40%. The rest of the time they feel and therefore behave as though they are a victim of the circumstances created by the people around them.

One example of this was when I worked on vision development with a team from a large corporate. They kept saying that they felt they needed an assertiveness workshop because they had a lot of 'unhealthy competitiveness' within their team. It was their belief that if they learned to talk more openly and honestly about how they really thought and felt about issues they could deal with this competitiveness more effectively. I suggested that this was totally unnecessary to deal with this problem because all they needed to do was for each of them to make the choice that they would no longer behave in a way that was unhealthily competitive! My suggestion was greeted by stunned silence!

You see, they were simply not taking responsibility. Instead they were placing the problem outside of themselves. How many times do you hear people say that they have a communication problem in the company as though it is nothing to do with them but up to 'the powers that be' to design a new communication system? It may be that, after hours of research and believing it will improve communications, a new system is finally laid down. How much does communication improve? Probably very little, if at all. However, let us suppose instead that everyone in the company decided that they were each going to take 100% responsibility for their own effective communication – would you need a new system at all?

Another way of looking at this is to imagine that you have a shop floor worker, who, when asked what his job is replies 'Well, I sweep the floor daily and when it is dirty I sweep it again', and that is the perspective that he has on his job. He sweeps the floor, earns his money and goes home at the end of each day. Another perspective could be 'I am responsible for seeing that this floor is immaculate at all times so that no dust gets into any of the products and we support our sales team in delivering top quality to our customers'. The first response is no more than a task orientation and the second approach is taking responsibility and having a purpose for doing the job. In training terms, what use would it be to give him more skills training to sweep the floor more effectively – in reality probably very little. Yet considerable amounts of money are spent on skills training. Without teaching and supporting responsibility and purpose I believe the training has limited ability to last.

I think, therefore, that the time has come to address training from a really different perspective – it needs to move more towards the development of the whole individual rather than purely the provision of skills. The mark of outstanding leadership is not just about being an outstanding leader it is about developing other leaders, even if they are colleagues, bosses, friends and family. It is about educating each person in our organisation to truly take responsibility for the overall success of their company and their part within it. If we concentrate on developing the whole person, helping them to understand the real meaning of taking responsibility, they can become truly empowered. They will have greater control of their own lives and the ability to develop and support others. In the situation we are beginning to find ourselves in – a possible recession, this way to look at things is even more critical, for each person needs to be able to find meaning and take responsibility for delivering the most outstanding performance they can – and this does not come by teaching them to be more skilful – it comes from engaging their hearts and minds – taking true responsibility.

The measurable evidence that we currently have through working with our clients over the last few years illustrates that this approach can improve performance dramatically and quickly, improve the lives of the individuals, significantly reduce stress levels and create a dramatically different and happier workplace. This engenders greater creativity and innovation, leading to better decisions in business and life.

In summary, although I know some training professionals are beginning to adopt a different perspective, I would ask the question 'is it happening fast enough to support the changing needs of business?' I believe that the total development of the individual, focusing on encouraging true responsibility is the foundation for real progress in other key areas such as empowerment and diversity, and work/life balance. It is impossible to teach these things without starting with the inside out approach. It is about caring and supporting each person to become the best they can be, it is about inspiring and listening rather than telling, giving rather than getting, supporting others to find their own way rather than telling them yours and about stimulating them to find their own motivation. This is true empowerment.

An example of the impact this approach can have was recently described by one of our clients, Glen Robson, Engineering Director of Sun Microsystems Inc, 'I found these ideas to be the most influential I have experienced during my career. I gained a new insight into teamwork, personal interaction and leadership. Additionally, the fact that the entire UK engineering management team adopted these principles, gave us a joint understanding of a better way of leadership. The effects both on our own behaviours and on the level of positive response we received from our teams, was little short of astonishing'.

How many people in your organisations are taking 100% responsibility for their individual success and happiness and 100% responsibility for the success and happiness of the company in which they work?

....

Succession planning

Companies taking an ad hoc approach to people issues can expect to lose out. Analysts Judith Scott and Darren Bagwell at US Stockbroker Robert Baird and Co suggest that whereas the last decade saw an obsession with Customer Relationship Management, technology enabled advancements in supply chain management and a focus on maximising service levels, global competitiveness and return on capital, the next issue is already with us – that of human capital management. They suggest that in this century access to human talent will be the most critical determinant of corporate success. Add to that a global skills shortage and increasing mobility of the workforce and no wonder that McKinsey Consulting recently declared that companies are increasingly engaged in a 'war for talent'.

Watson Wyatt add to this by emphasising that when a company pushes training for the next job, rather than how to succeed in the present post, it makes investments that other organisations – usually competitors – will recoup.

Outsourcing succession planning can bring an objectivity, simplicity and flexibility to a process often overlooked or biased when carried out internally.

The succession planning will include individual career maps, which incorporate personal development through various roles, related skills and internal progression strategy with development options. Emotive issues to be addressed surround grade structures, pressure on grades and banding to deliver salary expectations, grade drift, grade progression becoming the main career objective and the rigid confines of market based pay philosophies and employment legislation around human rights and equal opportunities.

Succession planning is usually carried out for senior levels in the organisation, e.g. main and subsidiary boards, senior and middle managers, and functional specialists. Areas often missed include key project workers and the hubs of the wheel, the CEO's personal assistant, the tea lady with 20 years' service, the unseen people without whom the organisation would function less effectively. Even small companies should consider this area, which is perhaps even more important for them, e.g. the MD's son may not be the best person to take over if the company is going for growth. These situations need careful, sensitive and objective management otherwise there will be a loss of performance when the time for change arrives.

In depth audits can be carried out in this area and service providers will need to be trusted with confidential strategic information. Key responses will include:

- What is the future operating environment for the company?

- What skills and talent do we have now and what will be needed in the short and mid term?

- How do we currently measure performance?

- What are our policies on internal investment in development versus buying in of skills?

- How do we currently identify and value our best people?

- Do we recruit for current need or potential?

- How would we identify potential?

- What does success look like?

There are few specialists in succession planning. The best organisations to approach are the occupational psychologists who also have experience in organisational design and as with other HR outsource providers, references and proven outputs are key in the selection process. This becomes more of a consultancy, advisory and specialist measurement service than an outsourced task.

The big issue currently is around identifying future leaders. This evolves from an understanding that leadership is key to the success of the organisation, knowing what leadership is and what it is to experience it, and how to incentivise and reward leadership behaviour. The issue when outsourcing succession plan is that leadership is based on a set of observable behaviours. Once defined the organisation needs to ensure these are practised until mastered and reinforced. This means a systematic process must be in place to feedback on the experience of these behaviours in others to the succession planners.

What we are discussing here is a competency model, development programme and 360 degree feedback process around the three basic components, inspiration, credibility and belief along with a good dose of intuition.

The outsource provider also has to understand that identification and development processes are no good without supporting mechanisms and will therefore have to build in coaching and feedback, goal identification and review, promotion and compensation plans and work closely with the client to align these with the business to ensure consistency of message and application.

The succession planning process

- Identifying the need.

- Consulting and sharing with line management, Directors and strategists about future direction of the organisation and key roles.

- Consulting with line management and Human Resources about role holders, retirements, end of assignment, potential high fliers, skills and capability etc.

- Data collation, HR audit, gap analysis and recommendations.

- Focus group agreements on reality and decisions to be taken.

- Personal development plans and mentoring schemes devised for appropriate candidates.

- Secondment activities set up as part of development process.

- On going coaching, feedback and communications, evaluation and reviews.

- Implementation of succession plans as appropriate.

Outplacement and employee assistance programmes

The main advantage of outsourcing outplacement is the access to full time professionals who provide an unemotive support to individuals in times of need. They also have skills that the organisation may not have in-house or may be used to applying in a different way. Also there can be conflict in that the project managers from the HR function for the dismissal or redundancy programme may also be the same people involved in providing an in-house outplacement service.

One main issue is that most outplacement providers work on a fee per candidate and therefore are not motivated to engage in the highest level of support as they would erode their margins. Suggested responses to this are manage outplacement programmes on retainer fees, output related bonuses, specific service level agreements describing number of hours of support, resources available etc.

Some outplacement providers sub contract their services and therefore pre-screening is to be encouraged. Also, where there are large numbers of employees being laid off, outplacement providers should be asked to visit the premises, work with relevant people on site and provide briefing sessions followed by drop in surgeries.

Rebate on contract is a useful area to consider. In one case where a sales director was placed with an outplacement provider at an agreed fee of £5,500 support over a three month period, he gained new employment after one week. The integrity of the provider in terms of their contractual terms allowed a rebate of £4,000 to the placing employer, thus guaranteeing future business.

Employee assistance programmes (EAP) are generally outsourced for several reasons:

- Stress and pressure are unpredictable and result in peaks and troughs of workload.

- Confidentiality.

- Cost of employing relevant professional experts.

- Experts become overly friendly, biased within one organisation.

- Sheep dip approach can happen as a result of internal policy.

- Different skills and knowledge are needed for different types of stress, e.g. workplace, personal relationships, financial and psychological.

There are varying parts to a true employee assistance programme, which can be co-ordinated through one provider or outsourced separately. These will include:

1. Risk assessment and referral: where employees have immediate access to a help line, through which the provider can gain information and suggest solutions, which are confidential to the employee. While they will not break confidences, the provider will issue trends reports back to the employer so an early warning signal is built in to anticipate pressure points where workplace stress is involved, or even serious interpersonal issues such as harassment or bullying. The good provider will clearly and transparently contract with each and every employee referred so that there is no doubt as to what is and what is not reported back to the employer. This should be covered both at briefing meetings (see 2) and again at the initial contact of the individual.

2. Training programmes both for management in terms of crisis response and stress avoidance, and for all employees in terms of managing themselves, coping strategies and self assessment of own mental state. The training will also include briefing on how and when to access and use support services. Building the confidence and security in the participating employees is crucial to success. The briefing content should not be underestimated and should include: personal introductory letter, brochures outlining the service, posters, videos, intranet based information, audio tapes as well as the actual briefing. Examples of the use of EAP in other organisations with case studies will also help. The provider should appeal to all the sensory representations when educating the client's employees so that no opportunity to

inform is lost. The client should check this is included both at the start of the contract and on an ongoing basis for new or transferred employees when setting up the service level agreement.

3. Specialist help: this can be for personal or work related crisis, where an employee just cannot cope any more. It should be available 24 hours a day and 365 days a year and will often determine the size of the EAP provider being contracted with. This will include legal service, health and mental health specialist, addiction problems, child and dependant care, marriage and relationship problems etc.

4. Short term help and advice: e.g. childcare, bereavement, disability issues.

5. Referral and assistance, e.g. where the provider does not have the specialist help but has a database of appropriate service providers. Again this can be short or long term and some companies offer this through a concierge service, which included domestic activities such as dog walking, elder care, interim nannies, travel arrangements, through to counselling and mediation, social services support, health issues etc.

6. Trauma management: these are more project based where the provider will supply an expert project team to come in and deal with a workplace trauma, e.g. fire, flooding, murder of a fellow employee, armed robbery, company bankruptcy etc. The team will deal with the immediate scenario and then provide ongoing follow through until resolutions are reached for each and every individual.

In each of the above scenarios confidentiality is absolutely crucial. Once this is lost with one employee the contract with the provider may as well be terminated as the usage will decline and the organisation will not only be wasting money but may well incur costs through unmanaged stress which manifests itself through absenteeism, higher employee turnover, accidents, decreased motivation and reduced productivity. A break clause should be built into the contract regarding confidentiality and database management. There is also a vast amount of legislation to be adhered to.

The client should have a published policy in the employee handbook on the use of the EAP and should also establish measurement criteria with the provider. In addition to the trends reports mentioned earlier, statistics regarding take-up, number of contacts per employee, long term activity, types of request etc. should be covered. Like other outsource providers there should be regular review and in this case where there is a large amount of usage a project team should be set up, possibly including the health and safety director, the company doctor, the head of human resources and an appropriate employee representative. The purpose of this team would be to review usage and make recommendations for improvement internally as required.

Areas to consider in EAP service level agreements

- Qualifications and expertise of providers employees;

- Professional indemnity cover;

- Supervision arrangements for counsellors etc;

- Types of service offered;

- What constituents are of each;

- 24 hr x 365 days per year cover;

- Multilingual provision;

- How are employee assessments carried out;

- Confidentiality agreements;

- Client feedback reports, content and frequency;

- Content of briefing and training sessions;

- Measurement of quality of counsellors and specialists;

- Follow up processes;

- Provision for client's new employees;

- Costing, subscription or transactional.

Coaching and coach training

The following case study challenges the thought processes in terms of insourcing, outsourcing and co-resourcing and has been included as a totally integrated example of what can be achieved when all three elements are successful.

Case study:
The best kept secret in Tunbridge Wells

Hidden behind a magnificent cedar tree, is the MCL Group, the company which owns Mazda Cars (UK) Ltd, where a state of the art coaching programme has been enabling employees to cope with cultural change within the turbulent UK car market.

Sally Vanson, Head of Human Resources and Charles Brook, an ex international sports coach and now Director of Performance First Ltd, devised the scheme. The business objective was to enhance the performance of employees (and therefore the bottom line) by allowing them to fully utilise their potential through a change from 'old motor industry' patriarchal management style to a new collegiate culture where freedom, awareness and responsibility allowed employees to leap out of their comfort zones and take ownership for a business that was starting to face challenging trading conditions.

Key to the success of the programme was gaining buy-in from the Board, providing an experience that was fun and high energy, would be owned by the line managers and where application of the new skills would be sustainable. One outcome was that managers should adopt a 'coaching style' to their people management practices to complement that of leader/manager. Another was that managers would be able to coach cross functionally. A key part of the philosophy was that coaching was non-directive, focused on effective processes and shared goals and that the model could be used as part of the daily operational routine in the business. Delivery of the training programmes was outsourced.

A highly interactive pilot programme was run for directors, focusing on sporting metaphors (golf and tennis) built on the Tim Galeway, Inner Game techniques, which demonstrated the non-directive GROW model (Goals, Reality, Options, Will). The sporting theme enabled understanding of the practical application with immediate and visual results.

What resulted allowed for the training of all who managed anyone to attend a 2-day coaching skills programme, which was then followed up through practice with a friendly 'buddy' chosen from co-delegates. After eight weeks delegates then attended a half day surgery (outsourced facilitation) to share best practice, discuss any issues and review how coaching skills were being used in the business, e.g. performance review, meetings management, sales discussions.

Having been supported through their learning, delegates worked to achieve a unit of competence, which demonstrated the application of the new knowledge back at work. Two hundred people went through the programme. Assessment of the competence was done by line managers and delegates and assessors were trained and accredited through an outsourced accreditation provider linked to the NVQ process.

Those coaches who were identified as having a particular empathy with people and affinity with the coaching concept were then 'invited' to become 'supercoaches'. This involved a two module '5' day programme, which covered advanced coaching techniques, introduction to neuro-linguistic programming as well as business application. The role of the 'supercoach' who is chosen from the line, is to support coaching and the coaches in the business.

A further level of support was provided through a bank of external executive coaches (managed by the outsource provider), who were able to demonstrate good practice, coach senior executives to improve performance, provide occasional remedial coaching if required and feedback on trends as they observed them as well as providing a level of supervision for the 'supercoaches' if required. At the top of the model, Sally Vanson and Charles Brook are continually updating their own skills and knowledge to provide constant and continuous improvements to the process so that it continues to evolve with the changing culture and is a truly evolving partnership of outsourced activity integrating with internal specialisms and expertise.

In the 15 months that the programme has been run, Mazda Cars (UK) has seen higher productivity, self reliant teams, a better quality of life at work, managers gaining time and less stress all round. The programme has been supplemented with team coaching (using internal and external coaches) which has linked to operational business planning and review activities, planning of key projects and the collegiate bonding of teams to fight their corner in the marketplace. Employees are supporting each other cross functionally and there are reports of using the process outside work to coach children in swimming and junior rugby, to manage life balance and in volunteer work.

Business benefits which are directly attributable to the programme include: the saving of £180,000 after a ten minute coaching conversation (covering the cost of the whole coaching programme in that division), the achievement of ISO 9000 through coaching employees so that they owned the processes, and a reduction in disciplinary conversations as employees take responsibility for their own performance. The quality of performance management has improved ten fold as individuals own the process and pull support from their managers in order to transform their outputs.

Success has not stopped here. The line has demanded a key follow-up programme for 2000. 'Positive Influencing Skills for a Changing World' covers issues such as giving and receiving feedback, communication skills, networking and negotiating.

To sum up, some comments from Mazda delegates:

'Coaching allows me to discover what I am really able to achieve and the reason I was employed – often before the words come out of my mouth'.

'The secret of coaching is to be with the coachee and enable him to discover what creative resources he has within himself'.

'Taking enormous risks both by asking and answering questions often gets amazing and spontaneous results. A coaching session can take 30 seconds if you get the question right'.

....

Administration of payroll, compensation and benefits

The administration of payroll and associated services is mainly calculative and financially based. Sometime this can operate from within the finance function as opposed to HR and explains why many HR departments have their roots within the financial areas of their organisations and often still report through the finance director.

The payroll function follows the legislation of the Income Tax (Employments) Regulations 1993 and other Acts relating to the social security and welfare side of the HR function – statutory maternity and soon paternity regulations, statutory sick pay, court orders, tax credits, etc. The overlap with other HR legislation, e.g. Working Hours Directive, minimum wage and holiday regulations,

P11D recording for income tax on benefits, national insurance liabilities etc. means that there must be integrated and aligned communication between the providers of the various activities whether in-house or outsourced. The payroll system and the personnel system must talk to each other as both will hold the same information about the same employees albeit payroll is about getting accurate information in and processing it whereas personnel systems are about getting the accurate information out.

Payroll is about meeting deadline, whether paying employees on time or paying the Inland Revenue. There is no excuse for missing these. Payroll legislation in the UK changes every year as a result of the Finance Act, changes to the calculations of national insurance contributions and debt collection and administration on behalf of the Government, e.g. student loan deductions, Working Families Tax Credits, Disabled Person's Tax Credits, and Scottish Variable Rate. All these changes must be reflected in the updating of software used, so the provider must have a robust and credible system with provision for annual refinements. It is worth spending time checking with the payroll provider on the process for designing and implementing the coping mechanism for new statutory requirements on their system, the programming routines and the involvement of Inland Revenue, specialists and customers where appropriate.

The system testing process is key and should be aligned to the test data and results provided by the Revenue and IMIS Software Evaluation Service. However the process does not stop there. Rapid response times are critical as for example in February 2000: the Inland Revenue changed its mind at the last minute by changing a rule regarding national insurance contributions rebate for employees in contracted-out employment.

Other changes impact on payroll through the management of P11D software, e.g. changes to taxation of company cars, reporting on carbon dioxide emission levels, introduction of statutory mileage rates, stakeholder pensions etc.

In 2000 the Inland Revenue, through its Payroll Support Unit, defined a set of payroll standards to address the payroll needs of small and new employers and to introduce an annual accreditation process. These are founded however on the need to deal with tax and national insurance administration and not the design of the systems. Care therefore must be taken in this area.

Cost measurements to consider when outsourcing payroll:

- Cost of production per payslip;

- Cost of production per payroll (usually monthly cost);

- Labour costs of payroll production;

- Cost of payroll system including upgrades;

- Consumables costs;

- Error trend analysis and cost of making good;

- Training costs re legislative changes etc.

Most payroll providers will offer a menu costing price model. This allows the client to add in requirements as and when required, however care should be taken to ensure the basics are included when setting up the contract.

These usually include:

- Calendarised payroll cycles usually monthly with standardised dates, usually the last Friday in the month, for pay received by employees.

- Maintaining employee database including starters and leavers.

- Employee database that is congruent with client's HR systems.

- Calculating adjustments from gross to net pay.

- Management of employee deductions including tax and national insurance, pensions contributions, loans, benefits contributions, etc.

- Balancing and checking payroll.

- Managing auto payment through bank accounts and cheques as requested.

- Printing off payslips.

- Delivery of payslips to site for all employees usually 2 days before payday.

- Balancing bank accounts.

- Accurate and timely submissions and payment to Inland Revenue.

- Automated system updates.

- P11D management with statements to employees for self assessment forms.

- Generation and delivery of P45 and P60 information.

- Managing, training and evaluating payroll staff.

The importance of getting the right pay at the right time is so important to employees in organisations that paying the provider on zero defects output related bonus should not be discounted as an incentive for quality excellence.

A major headache applies when it comes to the management of global payroll. This almost becomes a call or contact centre operation, open 24 hours a day to deal with queries etc. Global payment facilities are required as is multiple taxation management and dealing with global social security legislation. What currently happens is that the payroll gets re-outsourced to local providers. Data is managed differently in each and pay delivery and reporting is inconsistent around the world.

Getting rid of the headache becomes a major factor when outsourcing global payroll. The 'experts' will be able to flex their packaged solution to the employer needs. However care should be taken. Even if the provider manages to harmonise his/her systems with regard to taxation and social security, the political, financial and calendarisation of agenda will differ in differing countries. It would be too much to hope for that every country had the same tax year.

Record keeping and self service Human Resources

There are many and varied personnel systems to cope with the need to maintain the employee database within organisations. More and more companies are realising that instead of delegating the moronic task of voluminous inputting to one or more HR administrative employees, thus incurring cost and headcount, it makes sense to get individual employees to be responsible for maintaining their own records via the company Intranet. The task to be outsourced or not is that of system administrator. The co-ordination role is to ensure information is kept up to date, the system is robust, and updated regularly and that easily accessible reports can be collated and accessed simply and quickly when required and that these support the organisation's management information needs. Key issues to address are those of The Data Protection Act and confidentiality. Levels of access to employee records must be carefully thought through.

Added to the basic reporting requirements are the moves towards the paperless office, so this can become a complete document handling service linked to the scanning in of employee files, photographs, psychometric test results, and in these days of skills definition the need for video footage from interviews, presentations etc. A downside is that companies hope that technology will free them from mundane administration, but unless the users are experienced in the use of technology and formal methods of IT analysis, the systems will not be used to their full advantage. Research from systems providers show that only 40% of the potential from the systems is used.

The reality of the situation is that the basic information about employees gets entered on the system, but it is an exhausting and labour intensive exercise to collect other data, with little response from employees. It can actually cost more to operate the system than keep manual records. Specific areas of need should be addressed with the outsource provider when agreeing the service to be provided. Clarity should also be gained around professional Human Resources support to explain processes and guide users. Some of the IT sophistication has to be abandoned in favour of tools that line managers will understand, e.g. psychometric administration, online interview techniques, comprehensive job analysis, competence administration and assessment must all be simplified. This is a real chance for professional Human Resource managers to get line management to buy into the function and gain the benefits of a properly management people environment. This will give HR a sharper customer focus .

Advice to clients considering electronic system includes:

- Abandon preconceptions, start with a clean sheet, redesign the function, as you would like it to be, customer centric and value adding.

- Build processes, which meet business need with measurable impact through best use of IT.

- Work with the line managers to design systems they can use without training and add the features they want, not what you think is best for them.

- Get IT providers to instigate pilots and free trials, ensuring they take feedback. If the supplier refuses, get another one, it's not worth the hassle to continue.

As with the outsourcing of payroll systems the client must be clear about the results and information required – designing the positive outcome, and spend the time doing the research before making the decision. The responsibility for provision of correct and up to date information rests with the client and to outsource systems provision could result in a loss of control and effectiveness. Conversely it may be easier to get rid of the headache. The quality of the relationship with the provider then becomes vital.

The infrastructure of most company Intranets was only designed for voice, fax and lagging functions so there is an increasing demand for technological solutions, which are cost effective to solve the problems associated with the handling of audio and video material and even the slow delivery associated with graphics, e.g. photographs.

Many employers are suggesting that the self service or outsourced element of record keeping will allow Human Resources to be perceived as and be more effective at strategic roles within organisations. The quality and quantity of work that can flow through the latest electronic systems is a major advantage for improved communications and reduced administration, thus adding to the transformation of the Human Resources function. The driving forces behind electronic systems include improved HR productivity and performance, more effective HR service delivery, greater availability of technology and systems available and a demand for more strategic HR services. Surprisingly another key driver appears to be the cost control and savings element.

As organisations demand that Human Resources has a more valuable contribution than administration and becomes more of an internal consulting and commercial enabler, the line managers are responding by suggesting that Human Resources work is being 'dumped' on them. Any move towards self service HR must run in parallel with a line management education process regarding people management skills and responsibilities. Many system vendors suggest that line managers will become more effective at managing their staff since the system will provide more information faster, e.g. warnings about unusual absenteeism rates. Line managers however may feel overburdened as they already have their day-to-day responsibilities and other functions, i.e. Human Resources and finance ask them to take on board some of their tasks.

Potential clients should also understand that the Race Relations Act 2000, the most radical piece of race relations legislation in 25 years, will impact on the need for recording and monitoring. This provides for a duty for employers to avoid racial discrimination in carrying out any function, to work towards the elimination of unlawful discrimination and promote equality of opportunity and good relations between people of different racial groups. Any outsourced services have to be supplied in a way that is not discriminatory. The extent to which the promotion of racial equality is relevant will depend upon the function being carried out. This will require an analysis of policies and procedures with a likely racial impact, the completion of appropriate consultation and monitoring systems etc. The Commission for Racial Equality will be issuing codes of practice on how to deal with these areas. The provisions could have far reaching consequences on service providers. A number of developments are likely in the employment context when there is a statutory transfer of duties, e.g. a public authority listed as being under a duty to promote racial equality could be in breach of this duty if they do not take it into account when contracting out the service. They will need to include in the service level agreement an obligation to monitor. This transfer of statutory duties must be built into the contracting-out process and will soon include the monitoring of disabled persons as well. It will only be a matter of time before religion, sexual orientation and ageism are added. All of this will add cost to the design and customisation of personnel systems.

One argument for outsourcing systems provision is the attitude of in-house IT support. IT departments do not view Human Resources as a revenue generating business function and therefore response times can be lacking or unprioritised. For Human Resources people who join the profession because of a right brain preference this can become a nightmare.

The key advantage is the control that employees can take in terms of managing their own needs. Typically new employees are excited when they hear that they qualify for benefits as part of their new roles. They then have to be patient and deal with numerous contacts regarding pensions, medical insurance, variable benefits etc. They may have to physically walk through a building or even go to another building to meet the HR specialists who then become the experts on other employees' personal lives.

Self-service administration changes all of that. Employees have secure access to the website, which contains much of the information they need. Employee handbooks are scanned in for access on line.

Employees can do their personal maintenance, update their records, change beneficiaries, marital status etc. without having to go through the explanations required when involving a third party. This perception of increased privacy is a big added value bonus and one that is often missed.

One key outsourced provider has a portal, which allows employees of its client companies to check their accounts at midnight or midday. In addition it has hyperlinks to additional services that could be of interest, e.g. women going on maternity leave can link to home delivery nappy services, child care providers etc. When a client outsources with a provider, e.g. Exult, the provider creates a section of its portal for the client. The employees visit the site, which features their company logo and can personalise it any way they wish to. In addition they typically experience cost reductions. Exult is currently collecting data, but it assumes the 15% savings that IT outsourcing produces here and of course it standardises the way HR does things in every company. The added value is enormous. The client will have access to data it didn't have before. A company contemplating purchasing another can do a skills audit on its database to see if it already has the skills required to accomplish the merger.

An issue for the client to consider is that when moving information around the world at a reasonable speed, the technology becomes complex and network intensive, increasing the bandwidth pressure on older networks, and many clients do not have the infrastructure required to cope with this or to repair broken pipes and reroute data to keep the system effective. Consideration must therefore be given to ensuring that the provider and IT specialist work closely together. Some telecommunications companies, e.g. AT&T Solutions, will manage this from their client support centres around the world. Their professionals can tell in advance if there is a problem brewing and intervene before the client experiences any difficulty. Most problems occur when the client pushes the upper edge of the network capacity, which can be increased if pre-empted.

The benchmark for network uptime is in excess of 99.5%. This reliability factor alone makes it sensible to outsource the network management. Even though it may take six months or longer to get an entire new network up and running, clients can start using the system from day 1.

Expatriate services

Increasing legislation suggests that anything to do with expatriate services has to be managed under the legislation of the country in which they are working as well as that of the country in which they are employed. Every case can be different and even for global organisations it seems preferable to outsource the management of expatriate services which include taxation, pay ranges and benefits, compensation, relocation, schooling, induction, training in cultural diversity, language training, travel and property issues. The individual will also need personal financial planning advice, e.g. on selling or renting their principal home, taxation, spouse earning issues etc.

The key is to ensure the management of a fair and equitable approach to employees, which ensures they are neither better nor worse off than comparable roles at home, that careers are not jeopardised and that the organisation is not spending unnecessarily when local recruitment could easily fill the role in question. This is becoming increasingly complex due to the stress of living an ex-pat lifestyle. Language problems, work permits, visas, banking, family upheaval and the coaching and development support needed add to the difficulties.

Many of the large consulting and accounting firms provide the advice required, e.g. PricewaterhouseCoopers, KPMG, Towers Perrin, Accenture, Robson Rhodes etc.

Considerations when deciding to outsource the expatriate service provision would include:

- Current level of expertise in-house;

- Frequency of need;

- Back-up assistance available for employees when abroad;

- What does it cost?

- How up-to-date are you?

- Number of locations dealt with;

- Length and quality of support for each assignment;

- Feedback from previous expatriates;

- Is this really part of the core function?

There may be other ways of handling this. Some multinational employers have started to use 'virtual assignments' where managers use technology to handle overseas work. Many companies are using managers to run projects without being based in that country. Similarly part time assignments where the employee returns home Friday to Monday are increasing and not just in Europe, but commuting from China and Hong Kong is not unknown. This is mainly for personal and domestic reasons and reflects the increasing importance attached to family life and life balance as well as the explosion of two career relationships.

No two assignments are the same. Outsourcing providers have to be totally flexible in managing from a menu of needs. There also needs to be a more focused business case than ten years ago.

Expatriate activity management

- Assignment classification

- Assignment contract

- Policy definition

- Responsibilities

- Pre-assignment preparation

- Language training

- Spouse/partner/family assistance

- Networking and social contacts

- Remuneration

- Travel

- Freight, removals, storage

- Accommodation

- Cars

- Ancillary domestic staff

- Pets

- Education

- Pensions

- Insurance

- Leave

- Emergency evacuation

- Medical

- Communication

- PC, equipment, technology

- Repatriation

One of the key areas for the expatriate is the management of his/her personal finances. This is a minefield of complication involving the tax legislation in the destination country and the original source of income. There are also concerns over movement of assets from one country to another and whether taxation is relevant to local income or worldwide income.

Many of the large banks offer advice and services in this area and there is no point in any employer large or small trying to offer this advice in house, unless of course they are the bank!

Checklist for each element

1. What additional skill is available?

2. How will this element be managed?

3. Will it be task or the expertise or both to be outsourced?

4. How will the organisation maintain control of core function?

5. How will the outsourcing link to policy, process and culture?

6. What capital investment implications will there be?

7. How will software be transferred/supported?

8. What will happen in a fast expansion situation?

9. How will overflow be handled?

10. What flexibility is built in?

11. Who else is outsourcing these elements and what is their experience?

12. How will PR and credibility be enhanced?

13. What 'legacy' systems will have to be maintained?

14. Is this cost reduction, value adding or both?

15. How will performance be enhanced?

16. How much internal buy-in will there be by line managers?

17. What strategies are there around confidentiality?

18. Who is agreeing contracts and service level agreements?

19. How will outsourcing this impact on external environment and other stakeholders?

20. What is the real reason for outsourcing this element?

Motivation and incentives

The flexible benefits offered as incentive and motivational packages differentiates the employer and sends strong signals to the outside world about the culture and type of employer the organisation is. Giving employees the choice to choose and change their benefits sends a powerful message and this can cause administrative headaches unless outsourced. In the initial phase the client must be very clear what s/he expects to get out of the scheme and work on the transparency and equality issues.

An interesting emergence in the world of outsourcing is the provision of a 'human capital management programme' involving a bespoke employee benefits, e-HR and communications package. These originated in the US and are gaining popularity in Europe.

They work by offering a benefits package, which is seen by employees as dynamic and exciting and offer flexible choice across a range of 'lifestyle products and services'. There is an added benefit of an e-HR function which can be used in tandem with in-house HR services or instead of for some employers. The package is based on the web or company intranet and accessed by passwords which allow confidentiality, flexibility and the ability for each employee to customise their own website to deliver information on benefits and services that are important to them as an individual. Management reports give the client a full picture of how the site is being used by employees, and incentive points can be built in as a motivational scheme to incentivise behaviours, goal achievement etc.

Varied levels of access allow the tailoring of benefits packages by grade and hierarchy.

Revenue is generated by employer subscriptions (based on number of employees joining the scheme) and commissions from suppliers on employee and client company purchases. The package is not based on traditional Internet models, which rely on revenue through advertising, click-through revenue or a share of telephone revenue.

The HR services can be delivered in three areas:

- *HR News* – an online information feed bringing news, articles and headlines of all stories relating to HR, updated every 24 hrs.

- *Employers guide to HR* – an online guide to effective personnel management practice, giving essential information regarding the management of employees. This covers personnel policies and procedures, up-to-date legislation. It acts as a training ground for people new to HR and a reminder for the more experienced practitioners.

- *HR Marketplace* – negotiating special deals for HR related services from EAP schemes, staff help lines, stress care, e-learning, employee and office mobility, childcare provision and outsource providers

More information can be obtained from Motivano in the UK and US.

These schemes can also incorporate elements of the communications system that takes away some of the fears associated with traditional suggestion schemes etc. Network-based information systems are seen as more objective by all parties and creates more honest and open communications channels.

Performance management, linked to incentives, can be net based and allows employees to set their own goals and work towards them, tracking progress as they go. The benefits to the client include real choice in employee benefits, easy data interface and automated workflow with superior customer service from a standard methodology, which is tailored to the individual client.

CHAPTER 3

Choosing a supplier

Identifying potential suppliers

One of the key attributes of a provider is to be able to achieve, to get on with meeting the client's need as quickly as possible with minimum fuss. Often the empathy of the provider in terms of reducing the workload of Human Resources people through centralisation and standardisation can clinch the contract. This may be an unconscious choice of decision makers focused on cost effectiveness and compliance but nonetheless it is worthy of consideration. The sensible provider will understand that clients will have unique demands and that nothing should be too much trouble. There are creative ways to achieve everything. Once a provider has demonstrated this approach, the trust and therefore the business will grow. Goals change because industries change and the provider who offers client focus groups, think tanks either within client organisations or across others will add value and extend relationships.

How the client can leverage success

Clients are looking for the best of the best and the activities which leverage costing models can vary by supplier. These can be due to their varied backgrounds and experience, size and scale of their business, capital funding issues, quality and layers of management and overhead costs, operating models, value chains and shareholder expectation.

Ultimately the concept of benchmarking is key when deciding who to use, what to outsource and the methodology. There are four major sources of information available to the benchmarking team: desk research, use of third parties, surveys and interviews site visits.

Surveys and interviews and site visits allow the researcher to talk to employees of the alliance organisation, and so can be the preferred method, however in these days of mass technology there is much to be learned from carrying out desk research first. As well as web-based information this would include industry journals, directories, year books, professional specialist magazines, conference reports etc.

Third party information can be a wealth of information, but a reality check should take place to ensure awareness of professional egos and therefore not taking a literal translation of all that is offered. The quality of data collected is only as good as the questions asked.

Identifying potential suppliers can be time consuming. Some larger organisations may use an outsourcing consultant to manage the process for them. These people are typically supplied by the large specialists, e.g. PriceWaterhouseCoopers, Watson Wyatt and with large or complicated outsource activities to manage or where the decision affects more than one country this is an option that should be considered.

Otherwise suppliers can be located through:

- Chartered Institute of Personnel and Development

- Institute of Directors

- Other professional institutes

- Industry association directions, e.g. Personnel Managers Yearbook

- Speaker listings from conferences and seminars

- Outsourcing directories

- Yellow Pages

- Telephone directories

- Trade shows and exhibitions

- Outsourcing clearing house, e.g. The Outsourcing Institute, Brooklyn, New York

- Listings held by local Business Link

- The author of this book (sally@performance-first.co.uk)

- Local business networking meetings.

Although an outsource provider may provide a single function in an excellent way, this doesn't mean it can cope with the whole contract. Multi-functional providers need to earn their 'best in class' badge for their breadth of provision across a number of organisations of differing size, location and industry. This means that they should be evaluated on their ability to provide the services required through their people, their technology, their systems and processes and their customer centric management style. They should also be judged on their ability to invest in their own and the client's future. This requires a great deal of knowledge and experience and care should be taken to investigate their alliances, their funding and their resources, as well as day-to-day operations.

Characteristics of great suppliers

- Values alignment

- Evidence of quality management processes and commitment to continuous improvement

- Proven track record with reference sites

- Flexible, listening approach

- Reputation

- Customer satisfaction surveys/scores

- Shared approach to problem solving

- Commitment of specific resources

- Financial viability

- Proven management capability

- Expertise in handling employee issues, TUPE, etc

- Excitement and enthusiasm about the contract

- Thirst for learning about the client

- Customer centric strategies

- Cultural fit

- Cost conscious

- Willing to share knowledge and learning

- Fast and accurate response times

- Confidential and trustworthy

- Open book accounting

- Personable and approachable account management team

- Own excellent HR strategies

- Clear vision and understanding of their market and its potential.

Buying outsourcing services is rarely a comfortable experience, it can be like giving away the family silver. It's very easy to intellectualise especially with so much management information available but at the end of the day it's about putting the affairs of the company employees into the hands of a third party and thus losing some control. The circle continues when the buyer needs an expert to help manage the outsourcing process because the buyer doesn't feel s/he has the expertise, and the paradox is then about having the expertise to buy the best expert to assist in the process. Insecurity then becomes the norm. Further negative qualities can follow such as suspicion, ignorance, scepticism, feeling threatened and exposed and the whole process becomes so stressful that the buyer feels too tired to make the decision.

Choosing the supplier should reflect the fact that the Human Resources strategy must support the business strategy. Outsourcing provides the opportunity to identify any areas of non-alignment. The buyer needs to understand that some of the selection process will be intuitive and to manage the initial interactions in much the same way as a recruitment process. It is worth spending some time working out which clues would help to raise the confidence of the buyer at the beginning of the process.

These may include:

- Preparation, has the buyer done any homework, read the client company annual reports, learned about the business, found out who the main competition is and how they manager their HR functions?

- What has the supplier found out about the buyer, his/her position and background, motivations and aspirations?

- Has the supplier sent some introductory information prior to discussions. Is it concise and relevant?

- Has the supplier brought any reference cases, information about similar contracts, how they were set up, what worked and what didn't. How honest is the supplier about their processes?

- How collegiate is the supplier or is this a hard product sell? Is the supplier ready to share information and knowledge to help the buyer's understanding?

- How are the supplier's values reflected in the initial conversation: arrogant expert, patronising or listening and understanding?

- Is the supplier ready and willing to 'walk a mile in the buyer's moccasins', to see the world through his/her eyes in order to fully understand the requirements?

A useful notion to spend time considering is that of the perceptual position. This was originally formulated by John Grinder and Judith Delozier in 1987 as one of the early NLP concepts and is a model to use to enable an individual to take the perspective of several people simultaneously so as to dovetail the outcome for all concerned.

A perceptual position is essentially a particular point of view from which one person perceives a relationship. *First position* involves experiencing something through our own eyes (the client), *second position* involves experiencing the same situation as if another person (the supplier), *third position* involves standing back and perceiving the situation as an objective observer (fly on the wall) and the notion of *fourth position* was added at a later date as a term to describe the sense of the whole system or 'we' derived from a synthesis of the other three positions.

The basis for this idea comes from the fact that relationships always involve more than one person in the communication loop and the best outcomes flow from an ability to understand the ebb and flow of events that occur within the communication. Even when the participants do not agree, their relationship is enhanced and the possibility of future co-operation is created when they are able to shift position in relation to the interaction.

Perceptual positions

- How am I experiencing this discussion as myself (the client)?

- What is going on for me if I am in the role of the supplier?

- As a fly on the wall what am I seeing, hearing and feeling when this client and this supplier are having this discussion?

- Taking into account the knowledge, learning and wisdom from all three roles, what can we do to get the best outsourcing service there can possibly be?

There is a great move towards partnering with suppliers who work inclusively in strategic alliance adding value to the business. These organisations will have a full understanding of the client strategy and will own the policies, processes and required outputs in a seamless relationship with their own business. The relationship will be consultative and two way mentoring will be a key feature.

They will propose output related bonuses as part of their fee structure based on adherence to budget, shared cost savings or similar added value activities.

These suppliers will normally be tendering for outsourcing of the whole HR function, the more strategic activities or those softer and developmental areas. They will work closely with the core competences of the business.

Transactional suppliers will be more operationally focused. They will work strictly to a pre-agreed service level agreement, which stipulates detailed success criteria. Fees may well be charged on a menu basis or price for the job and the tendering process will focus around the harder HR skills, e.g. payroll and pension administration, self-serve administration systems, provision of temporary labour and traditional recruitment function. These suppliers are easier to manage as one dimensional service providers, will do what is required but rarely have the proactive culture to provide value adding activities to the client's business.

Whatever the relationship, it will generally start with an invitation to tender, a proposal as a result of some consultancy work, or similar formal process.

The organisation will also need to consider:

- Do we want a sole supplier or suppliers in each functional area?

- What else is outsourced and do any of our current relationships also have an HR outsourcing expertise?

- Would the current internal HR department want to be considered?

Forming the tender document

Anyone who has completed local authority tender documents for services to be provided will know that there is an art in ensuring that the information asked for and the responses supplied need to be SMART; specific, measurable, achievable, realistic and time bound.

Most suppliers will be aware of the significant time resource to be invested in responding to tenders and will be selective. It is in the interests of the client company to attract the right supplier and to be aware that the most commercially effective suppliers may choose not to respond to heavyweight requests for unreasonable amounts of information.

It should also be made clear to providers that they will not be discounted if they are unable to supply one part of the service. It may be possible for them to subcontract or work in alliance with another provider and this may be a better result for the client than the supplier trying to provide something that lies outside their areas of expertise.

Areas to consider when forming tender documents

- Introduction to the company, industry sector, turnover, number of employees, geographic locations, organisation charts, ownership and stakeholders.

- Type and scope of activity to be outsourced, current situation.

- Any employees to be transferred. TUPE issues.

- Length of contract, review and re-contracting process, circumstances which would force termination, notice periods etc.

- Penalty clauses.

- Full information re client's site – if supplier's employees to be located on site – security, health and safety policies, arrangements for access, parking, use of facilities, utilities, arrangements regarding telephones and equipment, upgrades, software licences etc.

- Client policy on use of subcontractors and alliances.

- Full information about supplier company. Size, ownership, previous e-supplier company's policies and process, copies of relevant insurance certificates, details of legal representatives, bank, accountants and auditors.

- Experience, reference sites (at least 3 other clients).

- Client relationship management system, account management, project management, specialist services and back-up, out of hours support, biographies of key contacts and employees.

- Briefings, communication and induction, how would supplier plan and implement the communication process to ensure ease of transition?

- Technology, systems, process integration and back-up.

- Project management, planning and scheduling, roles and responsibilities, quality monitoring and review.

- Client review process, how often, how much senior level involvement, tactical versus strategic input. Performance management process and measurement periods.

- Decision making and handover process. Who assumes responsibility at each stage.

- Due diligence and compliance, legislative implications and how these will be dealt with. Financial services compliance.

- Detailed break down of fees and deposits to be held including interest arrangements, pro-forma service level agreement, schedule of activities.

- How fees will be invoiced and payment periods.

- When fees will be reviewed and in what context.

- Agreement over division of shared savings, any output related bonus schemes.

Comparative proposals

Even though tender documents may have been sent out, proposals will still be returned in differing formats, using different jargon and suggesting different models for operating the activities to be outsourced. Often this will be a result of their own motivations for wanting the business, anything from available and unused capacity (more often in the transactional activities, e.g. payroll), to cost structures and understanding of the market environment.

A useful method of evaluating the proposals is to use a predetermined checklist, against which each member of the project team scores each proposal. This should be completed without prior discussion so that the team is not swayed by forceful personalities and an objective review takes place. Comparisons of findings should then be shared and areas for further investigation shared out among the team.

Providers will be keen to make proposals, which show their understanding of the client situation and ability to provide assistance. Some providers may overstate their ability at this stage. As the relationship progresses these proposals will become less formal and the client's need for comparison and competitive testing will reduce.

The simplified outline analysis by the project team could cover four main areas:

1. Identification of current situation, what is needed, when and what are the constraints?

2. What are the existing issues, what is the client trying to achieve, what is really going on for the client?

3. An expansion of these issues, some scenarios and solution testing.

4. Chunking down to a solution shortlist, outline and costings.

This would then need fleshing out with a strategy, which may take place over several meetings.

Making informed decisions

Most contracting decisions will go through three stages:

- Defining the need

- Reviewing all the options

- Finalising key issues and making a choice.

Sometimes the client's perception of his/her own need is unrealistic or not thought through. The good provider will assist by probing and chunking down to find out what is really going on and the results will meet the business needs of both parties, the client's personal needs and both come from an understanding of how the organisation works and makes its decisions.

The good client account manager will be working on three levels with the client. S/he will spend time discussing with passion and enthusiasm, their product or service offering, its features and benefits, while at the same time building a personal relationship with the client. Thirdly, the account manager will be asking open questions to find out about the organisation, its issues and complexities while actively listening to the answers. As the client it is useful to be aware of the process in order to manage the outcome.

It's worth the project team reviewing their decision making strategies. What has worked well in the past, how have good decisions been made in the organisations and maybe even benchmark these against the not so good decisions in order to define the 'difference that made the difference'.

There are three types of decision making process to be considered:

- Where one person makes the decision, often at director level, and the decision can be imposed often with little research and with time constraints on the individual making it. The chances of buy-in and commitment from other employees are somewhat reduced in these circumstances.

- The democratic decision, often made by the majority of a project team. This can be time consuming, needing several repetitive meetings as the convincer patterns of individuals in the team can differ.

- The consultative decision, where the key decision maker will consult with other members of the team and attempt to get advice as well as influence core players.

Exercise to establish clear decision making strategy

- Recall a time when you made the best decision you ever made, a specific time, could be personal or work based.

- As you go back to that time, what are you seeing, what are you hearing, what are you feeling?

- What was the outcome you wanted to achieve?

- What happened immediately after you wanted the outcome?

- What were you seeing, hearing, feeling?

- Then what happened?

- Keep repeating the last three questions until you get to the decision made stage.

- Review your answers and notice whether you needed to consult, gain further information, pilot or trial an activity, what motivated you, what pushed you off track, what were you feeling, hearing and/or seeing at each stage.

- How determined were you?

- When you have as much information as you can get, benchmark this strategy against two more good decisions in your life and note the commonalities.

- Repeat the exercise for a not so good decision and note what was missing or different.

- Review what would have happened if you had adopted the same strategy as the good decisions.

- Share your findings with the project team and agree the components of a good decision making strategy for the team.

Having agreed how the decision will be made, it's important to define roles and responsibilities. How will each member of the team be accountable to the whole team, who will keep and monitor the project plan and who else if anyone needs to be involved? It could also be useful to define barriers and blockages to the success of the project and agree how these will be overcome and how the positive aspects will be maximised.

The team will also want to benchmark the decision making process against the organisation's strategy and core competencies as discussed in Chapter 1 and ensure alignment. Some companies use the tendering process to obtain benchmarking information for improving internal provision. When this happens the client request for proposals should ask for clearly itemised information, listing the price for each service rather than the overall Human Resources function. This will allow decisions to be made around outsourcing the parts which are clearly cheaper and retaining the rest. This can be viewed as unethical practice and it is suggested that clients do not practise this often, if at all, as they will gain a reputation for time wasting in the provider world.

Part of agreeing the decision making process will be to define the key success criteria with weightings. Again the source for these will be the topics of discussion in Chapter 1, falling out of the business strategy and core competences. The easiest way of doing this is to list all the success criteria, link to strategic objectives or core competences, rank in order of importance and or value adding contribution, and allocate each a weighting out of a total of 100 points. The final list must add up to 100.

Table 2 Benchmarking the decision making process

Key success criteria	Link to strategy/core competences	Order of importance	Value adding	Weighting
E.g. price	Reduce overheads by 10%	2		30
Total				**100**

The decision(s) can then be run through the weighted criteria to get as close as possible to agreed and desired outcome. This exercise is particularly useful when debates arise about quality versus price versus reliability, or short term versus long term benefits.

It should not be forgotten that proposals have a hidden agenda – 'to sell'. The amount of time and effort to be invested in this critical stage should not be underestimated. It is key to check and recheck that claims about service provision are not overstated and detailed discussions held on findings before any provider gets on to the shortlist.

At the shortlist stage, the project team will be wanting to meet more of the provider's personnel. A good idea is to set up 'scenario challenge' meetings where both groups come together to debate the 'what if' questions about the activity in an open and honest environment. This may even include role playing potentially difficult situations. The time and effort invested in this will repay itself hundredfold further down the line. When the final relationship is in place and operating issues arise.

Topics to investigate at these meetings would include:

- Aligning the two cultures

- Vision, mission and values and how personnel articulate and live these

- Transferring people

- Contractual issues

- Grievance procedures

- Formal and informal feedback loops

- Open book accounting

- Maintaining brand identity.

Any worthwhile provider will at the same time be checking the client information and full and open dialogue should be taking place to ensure that the provider has everything s/he needs so that the final proposal can be agreed before selection takes place.

It is only when both parties are satisfied that the process should move to the design and contracting stage.

Creating value

The supplier company can add value to the client in many ways. Initially, there may be some basic observations about the way the HR activities have been run, which because of familiarity have not been as streamlined as they could have been. One of the issues about long serving and wholly owned employees is that retention strategies preclude new ideas from new people. The function may have become over cosy or cumbersome, so a complete review may bring some initial and welcome surprises.

Part of the outsourcing deal may be that the outsource supplier purchases some of the assets which are then leased back through the contract, e.g. hardware, software especially personnel systems. This is useful for the client company in terms of reporting return on assets, releasing cash for other purposes etc.

Another way a supplier can make financial savings is to share services required by a number of clients to achieve economies of scale or to enhance purchasing power.

Some less tangible added value measures include the releasing of senior management time for focus on core competences, the increased motivation of HR experts by talking to and working with like minded individuals, opportunities for development within their chosen field and another advantage could be the increased access to higher levels of expertise, especially in legislative areas, than perhaps one client could afford on their own.

It may be an idea for the project team to spend some time non-judgmentally mind mapping all the areas where the HR function touches the organisation and trying to define value adding connections before the start of the contract in order to link as much as possible into the scope to maximise positive impact on the organisation, e.g. one retail group who outsourced their HR activities and went down the self service HR route, realised the impact on their customer services and IT help desks of using the same process and procedures and increased the outsource contract to cover those areas as well, saving 15% headcount in the first year.

....

Case study:
The proposal document

- Our understanding of the current needs.

- XYZ has decided to outsource the retail store training activities while retaining an internal training manager to manage the interface between suppliers, XYZ and the stores, identify stores needs and co-ordinate the operational training planning activities.

- XYZ has asked Performance Outsourcing Ltd to propose what service could be provided in three areas:

  - to effectively manage and co-ordinate the administration of training courses to the stores;

The Challenge of Outsourcing Human Resources

- to provide a project management service for specific training/ development projects;

- to provide training delivery for specific programmes on Coaching Skills and Leadership as defined by the stores management team. (A separate proposal will follow for this work when requested).

The suggested timescale for this activity is to work towards a 1 December scaled handover, with employees being transferred from 1 January 2000 and a deadline of being fully up and running by 1 February 2000. This was arrived at after consideration of the budgeting process, staff movements and the need to get software and systems in place.

Key considerations

- Due to an XYZ organisational restructure there are some staff available who have an understanding of the stores, the manual and technological systems and relationships with head office employees.

This proposal is proposed as a result of a written brief from Mrs Bloggs to Sally Vanson and the Area Director has since endorsed this.

- We do not expect that this is cast in stone and would expect a flexible relationship founded on stores business needs.

- We would expect to agree a Service Level Agreement, based on the attached brief, and signed by XYZ Co and Performance Outsourcing before any staff were employed or work commences. This is to provide a foundation for measurement of key performance indicators or KPIs and to protect both parties.

- There is a current expertise within Performance Outsourcing, which covers the three areas of this proposal.

- Any intervention needs to be seamless and be innovative, creative and meet XYZ and shareholder values.

- Any intervention needs to involve bottom up consultation and participative design.

Training administration and project management

Our proposal is to provide a service as described in the written brief (client would provide this for attachment as an appendix).

This would involve the transfer of *3 members of staff* from the current Stores Training team to Performance Outsourcing. It would also involve the transfer of the *training record software system*. These people would be relocated within head office premises, with revised job descriptions and reporting lines. The project manager would also act as the Stores Account Manager and coordinate the interface with the Stores Training Manager.

Systems would be set up in liaison with the Stores Training Manager and a *formal review* would be requested at quarterly intervals which would cover content, methodology and outputs. Ongoing informal feedback, both verbal and written, would be solicited on a frequent basis.

Service standards would be pre agreed so that individuals understand precisely what is required of them in specific terms. They would need to visualise, practise and measure the impact of new behaviours and ways of working. These would include:

- the strategy, values and KPIs and how this is cascaded to the team. What exactly should be controlled, measured and rewarded;

- why seamless and differentiated customer service is important and how the success criteria are defined by the stores;

- what constitutes excellence in the relationship and how this is measured and evaluated by Performance Outsourcing.

The outcomes

Expected deliverables from this work include:

- Values that are shared so that a trusting relationship allows both parties to exceed expectations in terms of perceived service to stores network.

- A team of three who bring their hearts and minds to the project, showing commitment and loyalty to a business they can relate to.

- The dealers receive a seamless and consistent service.

- The relationship has integrity and authenticity as the external and internal processes and procedures are aligned.

- The project is cost effective to XYZ and a profitable relationship to Performance Outsourcing.

- Both sides manage the relationship proactively and commercially.

- The client manager will be Charles Smith who will interface with Emma Bloggs as the client.

Proposed fee structure

Financials

Integrity underpins our values. We propose working on a service-cost plus margin basis for service delivery only. XYZ will meet all operational and variable costs. All consumables, e.g. training venues, stationery and course materials, employee travel and subsistence costs software support and updating to be invoiced to XYZ at cost. Rental of any office space excluding Head Office areas would be charged at cost should these become necessary and requested by XYZ in the future. Additional employee expenditure, including temps, contract workers, recruitment costs, maternity, sick pay etc. would be charged on the same basis as the permanent employees, i.e. cost plus management fee. (XYZ would retain responsibilities under TUPE for redundancy costs should the contract be terminated).

Financials are projected to Year 2000 levels. Invoices will be submitted and should be paid one month in advance. Three months' notice should be given by either side regarding termination of contract.

Training administration

	£
Two full time employees	32,000
Payroll costs @ 27%	8,640
Merit pay @ 5%	1,600
Loan cards @ 960	1,920
Training @ 5%	1,600
Sub total	**45,760**
Management charge @ 15%	6,864
Total (excluding VAT)	**52,624**

Project management

	£
One part-time employee	16,000
Payroll costs @ 27%	4,320
Merit pay @ 5%	800
Loan cards @ 960	960
Training @ 5%	800
Sub total	**22,880**
Management charge @ 15%	3,432
Total (excluding VAT)	**26,312**
Total proposed costs	**78,936**

This fee would stand for year 2000, be subject to review where there are agreed changes to service levels and excludes all variable costs to be re-charged direct. Invoices would be submitted on a monthly basis phased over 12 months.

It is our policy to operate a value adding rather than cost down philosophy. Open book accounting also supports our core values.

CHAPTER 4

Briefing the outsource supplier

'Would you tell me, please, which way I ought to go from here?"

"That depends a good deal on where you want to get to" said the cat

"I don't care where", said Alice

"Then it doesn't matter which way you go" said the cat.'

Alice in Wonderland by Lewis Carroll

The expectations from an HR service

The first step on the journey is a step backwards. The client needs to know what it is s/he expects from the Human Resources service. The profession itself is currently at its most exciting, or from some perspectives at a time of greatest risk. Some Human Resources management do not have the power, authority or credibility to achieve the functional objectives.

The main Boards that do realise the commercial importance of people will be looking hard at their Human Resources specialist, and increasing legislation is also having an impact and making challenging demands. Before briefing the supplier therefore the client – whether s/he is a Human Resources specialist or not has a responsibility for selling in the need for whichever Human Resources activities are being considered by the organisation. This is a consultative selling activity. Too many internal management are product led, coming from a base of specialist knowledge and arrogance rather than building credibility by defining the business case. This is an opportunity to also define the perceived need from the employee or recipient's viewpoint. An ideal time to use fashionable right and left brain thinking. The logic of the left brain needs to be balanced with the inspiration, creativity and intuition of the right. The client will need to challenge limiting beliefs – has anyone ever said 'no', or is this presupposition self imposed?

The client should have a firm knowledge base from which to brief the supplier. This will come from total immersion in the annual report, strategic and business plans, department operating plans, knowledge regarding the outsourcing activity in general and information about competing suppliers.

Questions to ask

There are then some key questions to be answered before engaging in a time wasting process:

- Is work being carried out by Human Resources specialist, which with some training and development could be carried out by line managers?

- Are there any technically better ways to deliver the services before considering outsourcing, e.g. online training?

- How could some time be freed up to provide more quality time for the higher level delivery etc. consulting and coaching in-house?

- How can the challenge and fun of moving to a new and radically less bureaucratic HR provision be met?

- Could the internal hierarchical structure be replaced by a matrix or specialist/account management system. Could there be closer contact with the line management?

The decision to outsource involves getting the house in order first as part of defining the criteria for excellent performance. Briefing the supplier from a point of despair and depression will not result in a positive or improved result for anyone.

The client needs to have a clear idea of the desired outcome from outsourcing the HR activity, to notice what is happening and be prepared to change if the outcome is not being achieved, and have the flexibility to keep changing until the desired results are apparent. The results will only be as good as the outcome originally set. In order for it to have the maximum chance of working the following criteria should be considered for every stage on the outsourcing journey:

- State the outcome in the positive, it is easier to move towards something wanted than away from something negative.

- Play an active part and check how much control the client has over the achievement.

- Rehearse what it will be like when it is achieved, what will be going on within the organisation?

- What will be the evidence that it has been achieved? What will be the success criteria?

- What resources are available to achieve the outcome? If they are not already there, how will they be obtained?

- How appropriate is it?

Clients demand excellence from outsource suppliers. When HR activities are outsourced the net result must be better than the in-house provision. Supplier performance must be measured in three areas:

- More knowledge of the clients' operating business.

- More understanding of the clients' competitor base.

- Proactive contributions to increased profitability for the client.

The entire relationship can be reciprocal, each business becomes successful because of the other. Three dimensions are important:

- The supplier transforms from a service provider to a supplier of profits.

- The supplier supplies continuous added value rather than a cost effective service.

- Mutual growth is a key objective.

Well-formed outcomes will be easily achievable when the outsource provider lives and breathes the client's business. The provider will need to focus on:

- Customer centric team structures that combine interpersonal skills, leadership and decision making style and expert use of information technology. This will result in shorter response times and effective high value service propositions.

- A strong and well planned systems infrastructure which can process and produce inspirational reports on vast amounts of data in simple and readily accessible format.

- Alignment of strategy and goals which create short, medium and long term co-dependent relationships which sustains partnership and growth across all aspects of the business.

- Customer centric processes and information management which drive planning and implementation and creates momentum and innovation on both sides.

The interesting aspects of a Customer Relationship Management culture are that the client becomes better at sharing the organisational information with the suppliers. The more information the outsource provider has about the business, the closer s/he will be able to align the service to the need. Gone are the days when suppliers were viewed as con merchants and negotiating skills were about driving price and therefore margins down and thus negating the service quality in the longer term.

It cannot be emphasised enough how much measurement should be included at every stage. In any service level agreement the ability to make tangible measurements is key – *'if you can't measure it you can't manage it'*. However this could lead to an assumption and maybe a relief, that it is not necessary to have to think about relationships, trust, communications and the other soft skills involved in the provision of excellent service.

Some areas to investigate will include:

- Client responsibilities

- Business performance

- Provider performance

- Project performance

- The success of the relationship

- Customer satisfaction

- The role of the account manager.

For each of these it is worth identifying the vision – *if this is working well for both parties what will we be seeing, hearing and feeling? What will be happening?*

The big challenge at the moment is about behavioural change in the client organisation both at individual and team level. Trust and sharing are becoming paramount. The client needs to develop beyond current work practices and risk the new world. For example, to be able to access and utilise the information that suppliers are providing on the Internet, to educate themselves as to the best possible solutions for their organisations. Self service HR is a trend leader in this area. Employers can gain more information about benefits providers than ever and therefore purchase services that meet their own needs and expectations.

Building rapport

Positive relationship management for mutual benefit is therefore a core competence in the outsourcing activity. Developing influencing skills, which result in high rapport is well worth the time spent. To quote a presupposition from Neuro Linguistic Programming: *'the meaning of your communication is the response you get'*. Every effort should be made to develop a comfort and ease so that everyone involved in the outsource programme knows and understands what is being communicated and is fully conscious of the effects of their chosen communication so that an atmosphere of trust, confidence and participation evolves within which everyone responds freely.

Part of the trust building comes from shared values. Values embody what is important to both client and outsource provider and are supported by beliefs. They are acquired from experiences and from modelling other organisations, are related to the identity of the organisation and become the principles it lives by. These values will give motivation and direction and the most lasting values are chosen freely and not imposed. When considering the outsourcing relationship it may be of use to discover how the company values have been arrived at. Espoused values (top down) are usually not well lived and where different from those of the employees, can result in the company only employing half a person if that person has values that are incongruent with those of his/her employer. Supplier companies who have spent time and effort on values work with their employees, tend to understand the value of psychological contracts and develop long lasting relationships with their people who in turn care for their work.

Trust, confidence and the building of rapport are key to success and are often underestimated because they are difficult and uncomfortable to measure. This is where 'gut' is an important contributor. The client will have a gut feel about honesty, reliability, ethics and moral values and this should be given credence as part of the selection process and partnership building activities. This can be done early in the relationship by reviewing the small things: keeping promises to phone back, adherence to deadlines, persistence and openness.

The real sources of competitive advantage – knowledge, quality people management and motivation – must be chunked down so that everyone in the organisation understands, owns and contributes them in an aligned way. They 'walk the talk', 'live the dream' or whatever philosophy it takes to gain and maintain the emotional involvement that leads to a passion to give of their best and achieve the best they possibly can for themselves and their customers.

Both client and provider have to understand that being average is never enough. Achievement is about enabling people whether they be employees, customers or whole organisations to live their dreams. Being risk averse is a barrier, a blockage, an inhibitor. The recipe for success lies in becoming the maverick, seizing opportunities, daring to do things differently, trying and changing, managing chaos and complexity, always having something up your sleeve.

It is therefore worth the client checking out the provider's mission, vision and values statements and if not aligned, coming up with new statements that both parties can commit and buy in to for the operation of the contract.

The time invested in getting to this state of integration will be repaid tenfold when there are hiccups in the management of the contract.

Mission statement

Company A will work in a seamless partnership, sharing values with clients so that a trusting relationship develops and allows us to provide extra-ordinary service that enables organisational effectiveness and capability to underpin the client's business strategy.

Values of learning and growth underpin a belief that open, honest and constructive two-way feedback enables sustainable process improvement for the client whilst growing a flexible, creative and profitable business that our employees are proud to be part of.

Our vision

Our vision is to become the preferred niche supplier for small and medium size companies in Europe who wish to outsource all or part of their HR function to a dedicated team who will live and breathe their brand values, working as one with their other employees.

Our philosophy

Our employees bring their hearts, minds, humour and creativity to our projects, showing commitment, accountability and loyalty in a business they can relate to. We expect them to learn and grow with our clients and ourselves through challenge, support and flexibility.

In return we commit to being flexible, parent friendly and consultative whilst ensuring that all our relationships have integrity and authenticity and are aligned and managed proactively and commercially. We will cost all client work to ensure it adds true value to a sustainable, profitable future for ourselves, our people and our clients.

Our values and beliefs

Freedom	Clients and employees are free to choose who they work with and for.
Integrity	Sustainable long-term relationships are built upon honesty and trust.
Creativity	Being pro-active and state of the art enhances niche market positioning and continuous improvement.
Customer centric	Our people are also our customers. Happy people mean happy clients.

Stimulation	A stimulating working environment leads to continuous learning and fulfilment of potential.
Exploration	Helping our clients understand their true needs motivates our people and ourselves to exceed client expectations.
Continuous growth	Humility and listening allow us to grow our people, our business and therefore our service to our clients.

Having built the relationship and rapport, another key investment is to define and agree who does what. A lot of this will be determined in the service level agreement (Chapter 4) but the detail will be in the implementation stage.

Keys to success

The key to success is not in the intellectual agreement of who does what but in the personal commitment and buy in. Thinking about roles and responsibilities at six differing levels builds a useful model for shaping the content in terms of context, relationship, levels of learning and seeing each other's perspective. It also gives a framework for organising and gathering information so that either side can identify the best point at which to intervene if change has to be made in order for the outsource contract to evolve organically.

- **Environment** – where is the contract to be operated? What access do supplier or client have to each other's sites, what will be the impact on the relationship? How do the décor and facilities relate to the brand and what impact will the environment have on productivity and behaviour? How supportive is the environment to achieving the desired outcomes of the contract?

- **Behaviour** – what are the daily actions and routines that must happen, regardless of capabilities? What cultural behaviours are acceptable? What are the issues regarding dress code, eating at the desk, employee entrances and parking, social activities etc?

- **Capability** – what skill sets and strategies are brought to the contract? Where is the expertise?

- **Beliefs** – what are the shared beliefs that will inform the daily interactions? How liberating or restricting are these? Beliefs will influence behaviour, they will give stability and continuity and will motivate and shape the contract. High expectations will build competence and this should be remembered when agreeing accountabilities.

- **Identity** – whose identity are the employees to represent and how will this be manifested? What corporate resources should be adopted and where, if anywhere should separateness occur?

- **Alignment** – what is the purpose of the relationship? Why have roles and responsibilities been allocated? What is the fit with the greater system in the client organisation?

As already discussed, shared values can minimise conflict from the start of the relationship. When all parts of the relationship are in harmony the congruent behaviours will support successful achievement of the outcome. Where conflict starts to arise, the best way for the client to achieve his/her outcome is to achieve that of the supplier as well. Negotiating by dovetailing outcomes frames the activity as allies resolving a common problem as opposed to the 1980s models of negotiation through manipulation, which resulted in remorse, resentment, recrimination and revenge – a recipe for short term and non-renewable relationships.

There will always be issues arising. A good contract manager, like the good outsource provider will have the experience to pre-empt some of these and have people on hand to resolve them. The key is to communicate with all of the people all of the time as openly and honestly as possible. The role of the contract manager will involve managing the work processes through problem solving, quality improvement, benchmarking, and provision of hard, soft and experiential data. The role also involves leadership through focused and congruent objectives, continuous learning and team development, coaching, counselling and teaching, building trust, teamwork and collaboration, open communications, valuing and managing organisational and personal diversity, recognition and reward and cross organisational leadership and support.

Conflict may arise in varying stages of the relationship in differing ways. At the start, the client is secure in the process, not much information has to be shared, s/he is learning from and listening to the provider, there is little risk. The information flow is restricted as negotiating skills are trailed, and there are knowledge gaps on both sides. The relationship is low maintenance and progresses through personal chemistry and charisma, brand identity and raising levels of interest.

As the relationship transitions, there is more risk and more sharing involved. The provider now needs to move forward slowly, the client may feel threatened by the increased contact and much information moves to the open arena at this briefing stage. It becomes easy to adopt delaying tactics and play games such as withholding information to see if the provider is on the ball enough to ask for it. Sometimes this stage will not seem worth the effort. This transition needs to move into the communication stage as soon as possible. This is where values are shared, behaviour becomes open, honest and transparent and the partnership starts to grow. Familiarity with client processes, jargon etc. helps with the development of trust, however the increased flow of information, the speed of activity may also exacerbate the opportunity to 'do the wrong thing'. The client must still take care to maintain the positive and desired outcome for each and every intervention, to maintain control and to share concerns as soon as they arise thus minimising misunderstandings.

It is worth spending time here. This is the research stage, checking out possibilities and alignment, developing working patterns and too much rushing here could lead to short termism later in the relationship. This is where the alliance and partnership is built before the move on to the project team and the successful set up of the project if managed properly. Shared values will abound, shared concepts will be public and the security of shared goals will be a powerful focus for success.

Conflict can arise through frustration. If the provider is moving faster than the client, the client may feel threatened, the relationship will not be collaborative and eventually the relationship runs out.

The provider has been wasting his or her time and the client wasting his or her resources. The provider should be focusing on matching. Pacing and then leading the client through to a mutual consensus on conclusion.

If the opposite happens and the provider lags behind, the client will have to take the lead role. This may not be an issue if outsourcing a routine task, but where expertise or specialist input is part of the expectation the client may soon find him/herself having to disentangle from the relationship and find another provider.

Fun and flexibility is key. The whole philosophy of the virtuous service circle is founded on the belief that *everyone I touch is a customer*. Providing an environment for people to laugh and have fun means they drop their defences. Play makes it possible to be with someone at the worst possible moment and survive, to make mistakes and learn from them – a great diffuser when going through the teething stage of contracting out an emotive function such as Human Resources.

The client needs to be very aware that the first time outsourcing is used provides an opportunity to change the culture. To do away with cost and control structures and the negative focus that brings, and use inclusive partnering to add energy and creativity to the working patterns.

The provider will need to be briefed on working with processes not task. Control environments chunk down to low and work around tasks which employees find low level and demeaning. Combining clusters of task into one process means that roles get elevated and supervision becomes unnecessary because employees are trusted to take decisions. (Where they have been transferred the employees will have a greater knowledge of the client than the provider. The key is to build trust and motivation by enabling them to use it!) Checks, reconciliations and controls can be reduced by integrating the processes.

If the client, through the provider, measures results rather than input, the provider will be helped to focus on customer need and by organising the work concurrently instead of sequentially, will be able to re-engineer the process to add value to all stakeholders.

Sceptics will be looking to prove that the decision to outsource was wrong, and it may have been, but to start from this premise is to ignore the best shot.

Best practice

There is evidence that some organisations have saved up to 30% by outsourcing, with some of these savings coming from saved office space, lack of need to update or buy new systems and having people around 'just in case'!

The best practice for these people comes from the functional and strategic alignment of the provider's experience, technology and operating resources with the client's needs. The client cannot maximise this unless the provider has been thoroughly briefed.

To sum up, the briefing process must cover the following elements:

1. The establishment of the client company strategies, policies and procedures that will affect the provider.

2. Definition of new services and service changes, the design, development, implementation and communication of these services.

3. The allocation of time to implement the new programmes, deadlines, milestones and key success factors.

4. The management of contractual terms and invoicing, the accuracy and appropriateness of the invoices and time taken to review the services and ensure contractual terms are being met.

5. The on going daily management of each activity.

6. The development of management systems, especially those that provide the interface between the partnering organisations.

7. The provision of administrative, clerical and secretarial support for the monitoring process.

CHAPTER 5

Forming the contract

Which category of outsourcing?

Bill Lattimer, Head of the Outsourcing Practice at Andersen Consulting suggests that there are five distinct models for outsourcing:

1. Traditional outsourcing involves the transfer of people and assets to a company, which in return offers a service for a price.

2. A variant of model one, involves the client keeping ownership of the assets while still transferring the staff and service responsibility to the supplier.

3. The buying in of a management team from a supplier and giving them management control, while retaining the staff and the assets in house.

4. A bureau service, e.g. payroll, which involves outsourcing the activity to a centre, which also performs the function for many other companies. This would not normally involve the transfer of any staff or assets.

5. Various types of joint ventures are possible in any of the scenarios, which involve the transfer of staff or assets. It is common in Scandinavia for example, for outsourcers and customers to set up jointly owned companies into which the staff and assets are transferred – and to share the profits. The same results can be achieved by setting up benefit-sharing arrangements under any of the other models.

The service level agreement

There can be major discord between what forms the 'service' element of the contract, particularly when the provider has taken over the original employees from the client. These employees out of the goodness of their hearts, or through familiarity do a bit extra, which then becomes a lot extra and distorts the quality of output as measured by the client.

Service level agreements exist to protect both parties and minimise discourse. They should specify the minimum level of service that the client will get from the provider, should be jointly developed and drawn up and the understanding clearly checked out before signing. It should be relatively easy to evolve the content of the service level agreement from the tender and proposal documents, having refined the content along the way as a result of project team debates and discussion.

Often the service level agreement is a consensus between the ideal world view of the client and the realism of the provider in terms of what is feasible for the resources available – another result of the WIN:WIN approach. The client must ensure that the agreement clarifies what services the provider will provide and should include a risk allocation agreement. This indemnifies the client in case the provider causes a liability through failure to perform proper services. Provider audits should be included and the service levels should be fairly descriptive so that performance measurements can be objective.

The client's auditors may periodically review the function to see if there are any problems and the auditors would go through and look at all the policies and procedures to ensure they comply with current legislation. Failing this, the client could ask the provider for regular written reports on performance, and these would include specific information as to how it is dealing with action plans, grievances, terminations etc

As well as clarity and accountability the good service level agreement will encourage both partners to maintain a dialogue in order to plan for the service required in the future, be aware of the cost and resource application involved in any variation to service and enable the flexibility and awareness to cope with the differing scenarios of evolving organisations.

A good partnership will develop around the 'perceptual positions model' being able to see each other's world and therefore continually monitor, review and explore alternatives together, focus on the balance between excellent service and the cost of provision, understand the 'recipe for success' for both to succeed, and enable aligned definitions of the intangibles, e.g. 'as appropriate', 'as available', 'within reasonable time' etc.

Content of service level agreement

- Names of provider and client organisations, contact details and names and details of main point of contact for each partner.

- Outline of service being provided and site details both location and hours of service.

- Period of agreement and notice periods for both partners.

- Grievance and arbitration process.

- Ownership of assets, hardware and software, licensing arrangements etc.

- Legislative responsibility including data protection, TUPE etc.

- Responsibility for insurance for employer liability, protection of equipment and resources.

- Full details of the service being provided, accountabilities, responsibilities, timelines and measurement criteria.

- Qualitative criteria in terms of volume, accuracy, response times, presentation and reporting.

- Criteria re response times and decision making for non-routine jobs.

- Agreements for measurement, monitoring and client review process.

- Arrangements for contract review, re-tendering and consequential loss compensation.

Service Level Agreement

Proforma

1. *Parties to the agreement*

   This agreement is made on ... between a) ... and b) ... for a period of ...

2. *Purpose of the agreement*

   To include:

   – Overall intent ...

   – Scope ...

   – Exclusivity ...

   – Nature of intended relationship, to include general responsibility of each party ...
     – best endeavours ...
     – transparency of information ...
     – co-operation ...
     – accessibility etc ...

---

3. *Definitions*

4. *Conditions (for legal rigour)*

5. *Services covered by this agreement*

   Set out by:

   – Main service categories …

   – Details of component service activities …

   – KPIs …
     - definition …
     - minimum acceptable performance (vs. benchmarks?) …
     - target performance (vs. benchmarks?) …
     - benchmarking regime (if appropriate) …

   – Specific responsibilities accepted by client in this category (including timely provision of specifications, forecast volumes etc.) …

6. *Charges*

   – Basis of charging …

   – Rates (minimum, target, etc.) …

   – Period and basis of review of charges …

7. *General reporting and review*

    – Performance measures (KPIs + any other requirements …

    – Reporting responsibility …

    – Review frequency …

    – Review participation …

8. *Variations and queries*

    – Circumstances and process for varying terms of this agreement …

    – Responsibilities for handling queries …

9. *Disputes*

    – Penalties for non performance …

    – Process for handling unresolved conflicts …

For legal drafting reasons it may in practice be preferred that some elements of the agreement be appended rather than included in the body of the agreement.

There are also insurance policies available that can provide some security in the Human Resources areas. These can provide cover for employers in the event of a claim by a third party employee or subcontractor who may be deemed to be an employee.

These policies cover legislative violations, sexual harassment charges and wrongful dismissal terminations. They generally exclude health and safety claims. It may cover some claims in the benefits areas but would exclude pension or health claims that have not been properly paid out. It would also not cover punitive damages that are dealt with under general liability insurance.

··

Case study:
Outsourcing the store training and project management activities for XXX Limited

Trading agreement

This contract is made between the following parties:

1. **xxx** and

2. **yyy**

3. Appointment

Subject to the terms of this contract, **xxx** appoints **yyy** exclusively for the provision of HR Training Administration Services. The agreed fees for Year 2001 are £000 excluding VAT for services as described in the proposal. This is subject to review whenever service requirements change.

Duties of yyy

1. To perform its duties with due care and attention and in accordance with **xxx** requirements and in support of its business objectives.

2. To respond to **xxx** written briefs in a timely and professional manner.

3. Following *written briefs* to co-ordinate the production and purchasing of high quality cost effective services and materials which fit with **xxx** stated brand objectives and identity requirements, and subject to **xxx** approval.

4. Involve **xxx** in the briefing of suppliers as appropriate.

5. Only *commit to spend once signed purchase orders from **xxx** have been received.*

6. Hold *quarterly review* meetings to review performance and relationship from both perspectives, taking account of Store network feedback.

Duties of xxx

xxx agrees to undertake the following obligations to **yyy**:

1. Prepare written briefs detailing the requirements of each activity, to include targets and budget for all products and services.

2. Subject briefs to **yyy** to allow a reasonable amount of time for response, such time to be agreed in advance.

3. Sign off all budgets, invoices and supplier orders presented by **yyy** in a timely manner and as appropriate to deadlines.

4. Grant **yyy** access to all data records relevant to the duties of **yyy** and the spirit of this contract across all products and

services and assist **yyy** in the procurement of data records from its dealers, suppliers and business partners *in as much as this does not compromise any of the rules of the Data Protection Act, or compromise the integrity of any 3rd Party relationship agreement* **xxx** *may have.*

5. Conduct quarterly reviews with **yyy**.

6. Involve **yyy** as fully as possible in its training strategy development and planning processes.

7. Make available a simple point of contact, in the first instance the Stores Training Manager, for liaison with **yyy**.

Key performance indicators

yyy undertakes to operate within KPIs as specified in detailed written briefs.

Financials

1. An annual fee of £00000 excluding VAT will be *invoiced in advance to be paid monthly in advance* to cover the salary costs and management of dedicated **xxx** team.

2. Suppliers will invoice all pre-agreed and signed off supplies of products and services directly to **xxx** unless previously determined differently.

3. Where **yyy** is able to negotiate cost savings with approved suppliers, any such saving will be split with **xxx** 60%/40%

in favour of **xxx** *as long as pre-determined like-for-like quality parameters are agreed.*

Payment terms and expenses

1. Both parties at any change in levels of service will agree changes to financials.

2. Management charges will be agreed three months in advance of the beginning of each financial year, i.e. 30 September latest.

3. Any travel and hotel expenses incurred during the normal course of the performance of this contract will be charged to **xxx** at cost.

4. All operational and variable costs as described in the proposal will be met by **xxx**.

5. All staffing costs including redundancy payments, recruitment, maternity and sickness benefit to be recharged at cost to **xxx**. TUPE liability and responsibility remains with **xxx** for the duration of the contract.

6. **yyy** commits to measured performance management of employees to reduce **xxx** liability as far as possible.

7. **xxx** commit to an ongoing dialogue with **yyy** regarding health and duration of the contract in light of business circumstances.

8. Three months' notice will be given by either side regarding termination of the contract.

Confidentiality

yyy agrees not to copy, misuse or disclose confidential information or data to other parties, excluding those to whom disclosure must be made for statutory reasons or in the proper performance of this contract, without the prior consent of **xxx**.

Signed on behalf of the above parties:

For and on behalf of

xxx Limited

.... Director

.... Dated

For and on behalf of

yyy Limited

.... Director

.... Dated

Transfer and settling in

There must be a clear implementation plan that allows for an evolving transfer of roles and responsibilities with checkpoints and milestones built in. Different clients will proceed at different rates according to business context and cultural response times. Implementation plans should be simple and visual – possibly produced on Microsoft project or similar software with critical success factors clearly highlighted. Each phase of the plan will need a more detailed timetable and possibly some scenario planning so that unexpected incidents are dealt with within the plan and do not impact on future success.

Implementation checklist

- Analysis of circumstances and any alternatives.

- Objectives for implementation in line with business strategy, operation plans and client environmental analysis.

- Identification of blockages and obstacles, identification of key skills, systems, organisation and resources required.

- Business alignment and critical success factors.

- Identify implementation manager and team.

- Put in place training and communication processes for client employees and outsource employees.

- Implement new systems, processes and working relationships with allocated and costed resources to support.

- Prepare launch strategy, positive impact analysis and action plans, review and evaluation process.

The training and communication processes are key to the success of implementation. Having identified the skill, capability and understanding required for all concerned, the next step is to audit the current level of competence and identify the gap. This will lead to development of the processes required. The initial plan should focus on the ideal range of development and then each individual concerned should be reviewed against the whole plan in terms of personal need, thus resulting in a personal development plan for each. In this way the recognition of the uniqueness of each human being is realised.

Managing third party employees

As soon as the client company decides that there is no such thing as employee loyalty, they start to justify outsourcing. The good client however will self coach and ask him/herself whether it is that loyalty doesn't exist or that it isn't important within their organisation. Most will get to the latter and the provider can be sure the client will be looking for it as one of the unwritten rules of the contract. There are lessons to be learned regarding the unbundling of internal problems onto the outsource provider and there can be evidence that the outsourcing of employees actually leads organisations to resolve issues of employee loyalty in the process.

There are three key messages:

- the core objective of adding value to customers;

- doing this through seamless management activities that gain commitment of all concerned;

- measuring these through adherence to pre-set service standards.

First, it is important to define who is considered to be in this band of third party partners, and to reiterate the word partners because working alliances are key throughout the philosophy. This list is fairly representative of most large organisations, who may well have outsourced functions such as marketing services and call centres, joint ventures in areas such as financial services activity, and contract workers in support functions like cleaning and security. Most people will have relationships with training organisations and consultants.

One philosophy is very much aligned to Centre for Tomorrow's Company, which is the result of a three-year Royal Society of Arts inquiry into the measurement of strategic health of organisations and an inclusive approach to sustaining high performance. This framework focuses on the need to identify and share purpose and values and raise awareness with all stakeholders. It results in a balanced scorecard approach to measuring the business rather than relying on short term financial pictures, which have been found to drive a focus on instant results rather than customer needs or long term business goals. In short, success is about measuring what counts now, not what we have always counted in the past. Most Human Resources managers can quote or may even work for organisations which have enjoyed considerable financial success in the past and due to an inability to transform themselves are now suffering a rapid decline in their fortunes.

There is a view that setting output targets causes partners to behave defensively. The best example of this is in health and education where working to imposed goals causes unrest, and low morale often leads to inconsistent performance by undervalued employees. In trying to ensure that *all* relationships are as significant and useful as possible and accepting that failure and mistakes are occasionally inevitable the new corporations see themselves as organisations without boundaries and therefore expect relationships to overlap.

One push to move this philosophy forward results from beliefs about the future. There are predictions that the UK will become a nation of self-employed associates, that will have to scenario plan business backwards from a vision of where it may be, that anyone who believes he or she knows the answers is in for a rapid decline, and that practising humility is the key to learning and changing. It is key to clearly explain to suppliers that the relationship and task they are signing up to, may well not be the function they are actually fulfilling within 9-12 months' time and that the client may not be who suppliers think they are. Examples so far in 2001 alone include Autoflow, a logistics company which has expanded to include a fulfilment house, a Group Human Resources department which now sells recruitment, training and consultancy services and a retail company through a joint venture with Lloyds MCL which has launched its own credit card.

The Japanese heritage of Mazda provides a base for this ethos. Mazda is a product of the regeneration of Hiroshima, where the fight for survival has led to a strong work ethic and core values of customer satisfaction and integrity. When Ford took management control of Mazda in 1996 and East met West, the result could have been a mess. However by focus, talking and learning – harmony and consistency evolved alongside the harder science of cost cutting and control. 'Kansei' is the Japanese word for harmony, and it was this ideal that led Mazda UK in 1997 to commission a Double Concerto for saxophone and cello to demonstrate how conflict can be resolved. (The two instruments had never been played together in this way before). This wacky approach to cultural awareness demonstrates our keenness to promote an environment of growth and evolution in a unique and personal way.

For third party partners, there are have many types of contract and levels of commitment and trust. These do not sit easily within the confines of new employment legislation and professional responsibilities. Benchmarking by internal employees and other forms of measurement cause difficulties. Mazda has to manage complexity and this becomes a challenge for high performance. However as Walt Disney said, '*if you can dream it, you can do it*'.

Employers like to think they understand reality. Nowadays employees can only be promised that they will be marketable when they leave. Organisations fulfil this promise through a wide remit of personal development opportunities and should open these programmes up to third party partners. It is also worth looking at their employment conditions to check these meet some of the higher level, more personal needs than security. These would include areas such as working environment, behaviours, alignment with personal beliefs and values, identity and the larger systems such as family and community. We build these areas into service level agreements when outsourcing activities.

The ideal results depend on the way external messages are aligned with the way people and jobs work. There has been a move away from traditional HR concerns of process and procedures to a more marketing oriented approach with a focus on image, relationships, and communications. This maximises brand equity through absolute buy in of brand values by suppliers and assists the appearance of a seamless organisation where the join between the client and its customer facing partners is invisible and customer ownership becomes interdependent.

Current research tells us that in call centres alone in the UK there is 30% staff turnover. This reduces goodwill and PR and increases recruitment costs at approximately £2,000 per head. When outsourcing other service functions such as Human Resources, the client must welcome two-way feedback so that service level agreements can be matched to success criteria, and both share recruitment tools and best practices to optimise these relationships. In this way formal supplier management activities are complemented by informal regular review which enables both to speak with one voice. In return for this high investment of time, money and expertise, it is only right to seek support on the journey to perfection. Both partners should expect to give and receive instant feedback on many of the triggers of discontent, e.g. below standard product, increasing customer expectation, funding ability, buying trends and technology. It is only then that issues can be resolved jointly, adding value to the customer optimising impact on the bottom line and sustaining future profitability and growth through customer retention.

Thinking of another Japanese word 'Kaizen' – there must be continuous improvement. Everyone can share, continually learn and react, by being flexible, competitive and consistent. Research is now showing that third party partners look for affinity benefits packages, thorough induction, rapid promotion prospects and support for training and education. It is important, therefore, to get involved in their performance measurement so we can share in the response to these needs.

It is vital to share information.

Mazda

If the brakes on a car in the UK fail, the production line in Hiroshima will know in minutes. This use of 'e' mail and technology is essential to the communication cascade from Hiroshima, to the European offices to Mazda UK, to the dealer network. More locally, a request for a car brochure via our Mazda Internet sites, is passed directly to our fulfilment house who meet the customer's requirements. The customer receiving this brochure on the doormat is totally unaware of the chain of four service providers involved in the chain. This success depends on sharing knowledge among key players in the chain and understanding the financial and other needs and motivations of each partner in order to stay at the cutting edge.

We try very hard to communicate. We issue product bulletins; copies of press releases share our office facilities so partners are encouraged to drop by. We invite them to key events such as car launches e.g. last year's launch of the Mazda 323 in Euro Disney, and we cherish the involvement of partners and their families in our charity work, which varies from sponsoring Barnados over the last three years and providing work placements in dealerships for disadvantaged youngsters, to getting involved in a community play for the Millennium or simply planting a tree as part of our Future Forests Campaign.

At the Motor Show we gave wearers the opportunity to design or choose their own uniform. Corporate identity is key to providing a sense of belonging to the tribe. Everyone from insurance advisors, call centre workers to sunroof fitters needs to know what binds them as a brand – they also have access to the MD through a 24-hour hotline and can send in their suggestions by 'e' mail. We raise awareness and responsibility for maintaining standards through sports based Performance Coaching programmes, which are first and foremost fun while being used to coach in ever higher service standards. Partners are also encouraged to know about and to buy our products, and we make this easy for them through discounting both product and financial services.

Working with successful partners – the ones who are never satisfied – offers the chance to grow and succeed with our brands. It's not about selling services, it's about selling customer experiences – or in simpler words, emotional relationships between the buyer and third party partners. It is vital, therefore, to trust the outsourcing suppliers to make decisions about customers within the framework of service level agreements, to achieve these ideals by following vision and purpose. Sometimes it works and sometimes it doesn't. The key lies in continuously improving.

From a Human Resources perspective the client must role model the message they want the supplier to communicate – and treat them also as customers. It's useful to invite their account managers to supplier days, so they hear the ground rules as well as the business strategy and learn to work alongside competitors without fighting over contracts, to link gifts to the values systems and send them home with balloons, pens, tee shirts etc., for the family, to *try to make the relationships fun*.

It's also important to check that external messages match internal behaviours, e.g. an innovative product with innovative working practices, to describe to our partners what shared success looks like to the client, and to *measure their goals to ensure they are aligned with the client*. For example, brand values of 'spirited, insightful and stylish' impact on third party partners in that they need them to represent these by being well presented, intuitive, clever, sensitive and fun – imagine the challenge of testing for some of these qualities during the recruitment process!

A challenge is to try to ensure that training and development add personal interest and focus on interpersonal activities such as rapport building, body language, and linguistics so that partners grow in confidence and stature as human beings, and enjoy their own success, and to provide business and personal incentives to succeed through incentive schemes which, unlike many of their kind, don't forget those who do not work in the front line of sales.

This WIN:WIN relationship approach is based simply on *what, interest and need*. Successful relationships invest time understanding what it is that partners value; and trying to manage the partnership mix in terms of reputation, motivation, loyalty, trust, and performance management, then defining any gaps, working hard to close them, and continually reviewing the relationships through focus groups, suppliers' audits and most simply *listening, talking and feeding back*. In this way value is continually added, management is seamless and the performance of all involved is easy to measure.

Client review process

Formal and informal client review, ongoing evaluation and learning for both partners is key to success. These will act as a sense check, highlight areas still at risk, review worms and diamonds (hinders and helps), and provide information for line management focus on quality intensification, values, productivity, customer satisfaction and simplification. Informal reviews can be done by telephone, corridor meetings and 'e' mail. However, formal reviews should be built in at least monthly at the beginning of the project and no less often than quarterly as it matures.

The content of these will evolve, and a useful framework is to use a checklist for the review:

1. Overall summary of what's going on

2. Successes

3. Actions

4. Health check, analysis and reflection

5. New information

6. Where focus is required

7. Key messages.

Typical client review

How's it going for all involved, incidents and anecdotes, informal and open conversation.

Successes

- What's been happening and what's going well for both client and provider.

Actions

- Rolling business plan, short term 6-18 months.

- Status of relationship in regard to plan.

- Business objectives and impact on contract: sales, profit, lifetime value etc.

- Provider team operational objectives.

- Client decision making processes and contact with provider.

- Members of provider team, contact and response times and quality.

- Projects and activities in relation to business objectives with milestones and monitors.

- Action plan timetable with accountability and timescales.

- Resource implications: people, equipment, budgets, investments.

- Risks and contingency.

Provider's health check

- Profitability analysis.

- Competitive position.

- Vulnerability and uncertainties, actions to defend or expand.

- Client strategy and value drivers, the business experience.

- Client critical success factors and current performance.

- Positive impact analysis and screening, provision of evidence.

New information

- New clients for provider, contacts and activities.

- New products and services from provider.

- Both of above for client business.

- Current projects for both partners.

- Legislation, expected impact and need to resolve.

- New employees for both partners who could impact on relationship.

- Any other business.

Focus required

- Internal marketing.

- Communication processes.

- Implementation support.

- Employee development and actions.

Key messages

- Pro-activity.

- Visibility.

- Communication.

- Improvements/changes to be agreed.

- Next meeting and outline agenda.

Measures of excellence

There are many areas of excellence to measure. These would include:

1. Customer satisfaction: supporting common goals, effective service to line managers, support on personal issues, contribution to functional goals, communication of objectives and policies, support when implementing change.

2. Business results: cost/benefit analysis, management actions.

3. Employee motivation and feedback: consultation, flow of information, response times, proactivity, consistency and services offered.

However the two main areas of consideration in terms of how well the HR outsource provider is performing will be cost and quality.

In regard to cost, measures need not rely on variation against budget, but can be tracked by ratios against each employee and trends will emerge over a period of time, e.g. training cost per employee or per hour, recruiting cost per vacancy, per hour, insurance costs per employee, payroll costs per employee, relocation per mile.

Quality measures can be derived from employee surveys, not just the attitude surveys, but the training evaluation forms, induction reviews, recruitment reviews, questions asked at exit interviews etc. (of course, the administration of all this measurement could result in another activity to be outsourced!)

The key part of the equation that brings these two measures together is the supplier review meetings. These should happen formally 3-4 times per year, but a channel must be kept open for immediate and informal feedback thus building the trust and partnership already discussed as a major requirement to achieving excellent results.

Table 3 Critical factors in determining success

	Percentage of employers
Cost-effectiveness	61
Redirection of HR focus towards strategy and planning	55
Improved customer service	52
Higher level of technical expertise	48
Reduced administrative costs	44
Seamless delivery of services	40
Higher level of participant satisfaction	37
Stronger focus on core business	36
Quicker response to participants requests	22
Higher levels of accuracy	19
Increased flexibility in handling special needs	15
Increased understanding by participants	10

Source: 1996 Outsourcing survey, Hewitt Associates, Lincolnshire, Illinois

The levels of accuracy that can be gained, also add value to the cost reduction exercise. Research suggests that Human Resources employees spend 60% of their time on administrative tasks, filling out forms, changing records etc. Reducing stress levels by employing more people to carry out the task is an interesting concept, especially when the transactional activities, e.g. self service Human Resources systems, payroll processing actually take place remotely in countries such as India or the Philippines where labour costs are cheaper. This allows each client to have a dedicated team and a back-up team to help with peak workloads and cover sickness and holidays. The back-up pool also provides a training and progression route for employees who then get permanent work on the dedicated team once a role becomes available. Feedback from one US provider suggests that errors have been reduced from 5% to zero through this strategy.

Pricing structures and incentives

Open book accounting is defined as the provider giving the client a full breakdown of costs, raw materials and services. The client may also share their own costs of managing the service in-house.

It has always been useful to practise open book accounting. However this is not an excuse for the client to manipulate information to get price reductions and anyone practising this strategy is on a sure-fire route to break down the relationship. Providers with the most to fear from open book accounting are those who have internal costs, which are not customer centric, i.e. add no value to the client. These companies will need to work on improving 'value added' and streamlining their activities to take cost out.

Some honest providers may object to sharing through misguided notions of pride or privacy. This may be admirable but does little to build trust and therefore impacts on their position within the client relationship.

Providers who welcome the request have little to fear and welcome the client input. These companies tend to be open to learning and sharing and therefore build their business to mutual advantage.

There are no clear cut price ranges and the fees vary between services where criteria such as number of employees, options and location will affect the outcome. A typical outsourced payroll provider will charge between 4 and 8% of gross salary bill per month, and this may be much cheaper than the in house systems and salaries of employees. Outsourced payroll contracts usually run for a year and the sensible client will build in a break clause, either monthly or quarterly to cope with changing business scenarios or the fact that the service may not be up to standard. There are many costing models to choose from when outsourcing the Human Resources function.

- Cost for job: where the provider is paid a fee for the total service, usually reviewable annually and is often used for transactional activity.

- Output related: where there may be a partly or wholly variable element to the contract price based on achieving certain targets or levels of accuracy, e.g. zero defects on payroll, recruitment within time frame, etc.

- Cost plus: where the provider through open book accounting declares all the costs of running the contract and is then paid either a fixed or percentage management fee on top of the costs. This is more usual for varied and service provision where the provision is hard to quantify.

- Management fee: where the client retains and pays all the costs in-house and the provider is paid a management fee for managing the activity.

- Shared savings: where the provider is tasked with streamlining the function and gets a share of any proven savings made as an incentive to add value. This is usually on an annual basis and the share is 40:60% in favour of the client.

Pricing will not always be focused on the lowest price the client can get away with. There will be an element of cost: benefit analysis as the client will want to factor in value added, highest rate of return, long term economies of scale and minimal disruption to internal processes.

Hidden costs to consider in terms of pricing models include:

- TUPE and/or redundancy costs including transitional costs with regard to employee communication, coaching, counselling and consultation, possible relocation, buying out of benefits etc.

- Goodwill resulting from familiarity. Current client employees will know the internal systems, processes and people. How much knowledge will be lost during the transfer and how does this balance out against the gains?

- What happens to current client company assets used by Human Resources, e.g. company cars, computers and other equipment – are there penalty clauses for early redemption of leases, can these be re-allocated, will the provider take them on?

- Premises and facilities – if the provider is working from their own site is there a recharge for office accommodation and if so is this a double charge or has the client's own space been re-assigned or disposed of?

- How will any legislative accountability be managed. What damage limitation is there with regard to handing over responsibility for compliance to the provider? Who pays if there are legal issues to be resolved?

It is useful to remember that providers can make high margins and therefore the competition will be able to undercut on price in most cases. This is particularly the case in the interpersonal or higher skill service provision, e.g. Human Resources strategy, recruitment, relocation and management of expatriate services rather than the transactional areas such as payroll administration and record keeping. When competitors suggest reduced prices in these areas the client must be particularly vigilant in defining what loss of service s/he can expect as a result of lower margins. The professional provider will be using the higher margin to differentiate in these areas and the fact that they have this professional expertise available in their portfolio is an area to be considered when looking at Human Resources service provision and value adding outputs.

There are two key questions for the client to consider in terms of price for the outsourced service:

1. Can the client sell current assets as part of the deal and then be charged for lease back? This has the advantage of freeing up cash for other purposes as well as increasing the return on assets in terms of financial reporting which will have a positive impact on net worth of the company. This strategy can be useful to support financial strategies with regard to cash flow management, shareholder reporting, making the company more attractive to investors etc.

2. Can the client save money by using the provider's network to reduce costs and achieve economies of scale?

If the answer to both of these is no, then the client can retain the Human Resources provision more cheaply and will need to focus on the added value reasons for outsourcing.

It is useful for the client to understand the supplier motivation for the pricing model. Some suppliers may go in at a low base price in order to win the business and then price additional services at high margin and focus on selling these in wherever possible. This assumes that having got the core business, the rest will follow. The client will be able to avoid this by checking the breakdown of pricing models and asking for a menu of prices of additional services at the contract formation stage. This is fundamental in growth and diversifying organisations where the service provision is likely to change rapidly. Similarly, on long term contracts, the supplier may go in at a cheaper rate then push the prices up after a couple of years, or include early contract redemption penalties to compensate for loss of profits. The client will therefore need to negotiate break clauses at short term intervals, with minimal redemption penalties and although according to the needs of the business, this is where the management fee or cost plus pricing models are to the client's advantage.

CHAPTER 6

Communicating the decision and implementation

Energy, transparency and communication

There is no excuse for employees finding out through the grapevine that their job is to be outsourced. Trust is lost when they find out through other means and then become suspicious instead of inclusive. An important aspect of smooth outsourcing is to transfer employees with their morale intact and as a key asset in the venture their well being and motivation should be one of the first areas to be discussed.

They should be informed that outsourcing is being considered at the earliest possible opportunity, even if no concrete decision has been made. The communications should then remain consistent until the decision is made. Unisys Outsourcing advise that as soon as the provider is chosen, arrangements should be made to talk to the people themselves. Basically they want to put the human side to the transaction and understand that employees want a career growth plan and want to know that there is a very good life after outsourcing.

Case study

When Unisys get to the point of closing the deal, they have group and one to one meetings to understand fears, concerns and desires and are able to reassure the employees that everything will be taken care of and that they understand that outsourcing can be a scary thing.

Employees are then allocated to a support service within Unisys and a number of options given, e.g. relocation to a service centre, working from home or provision of assistance to leave and go elsewhere. Bob Evans, vice president and general manager, insists that Unisys manage by results not activity and therefore leaving options open ensures that if results can be produced they will try and make the options work.

Unisys also has a state of the art Human Resources system through which employee skills are assessed and entered onto a database so that every project manager and corporate manager in the company knows where to look for specific skills. The system also has a Unisys University to help employees understand what career advancement classes they can take. Career pathing is provided so that employees can understand what markets the company is in and the disciplines they have. All job vacancies are published and employees can apply for any job worldwide.

Bob Evans stresses that the career transition process is important and should not be overlooked because a company does not want to lose its intellectual capital, the most important part of its processing ability. He reinforces the fact that the company focus on the people themselves, understanding their personal situations, explaining the business needs and come to conclusions generally in favour of the employee.

The customer centricity involved with this approach means that the client understands that people who are critical to their activities are being taken care of and that the internal knowledge base collected over a number a years will continue with the outsource provider.

....

A number of studies have shown that giving employees some say in the process will boost the success rate of the project, through a more committed and productive workforce. Despite this, fear of consultation has meant that on average 10% of employers have consultative systems in place, and less than 25% of employers have works councils. It can be argued that this explains low level of commitment in some organisations. Other studies show that consultative committees make it easier to introduce change to working practice and improvements and productivity, through quality communication and decision making – all key to the outsourced contacts.

It does not have to be a formal process however. The nature of the relationship between the employer and the workforce, the culture and trust that develop are the keys to success and that this can channel the adversarial element in organisations. It can also be argued that the benefits do not just extend to the organisation, they reduce the stress levels that often arise through fear of the unknown.

The client will need to lead all involved towards achieving the goals in the best possible way within the system in which the organisation operates. This is very much about leadership – 'going first, guiding dance partners through the steps of the dance, leading the orchestra'. This leadership style is about 'getting others to want to do things' as opposed to the management style of 'getting things done through other people'. It is leadership that is required in times of transformation and change. Management is associated with establishing order, productivity and sustainability.

In defining an effective communication strategy the client will need to ensure that the decision makers' adopt the appropriate state, language, attitude to align themselves with the messages they want employees to receive. How often do we hear 'empty words' from management? – memos or presentations where the words are saying all the right things, but the body language of the communicator, facial expression, tone of voice etc. are not aligned and therefore the majority of the message is lost. Words are only 7% of our communication, the rest of our intent comes from our beliefs and values systems.

Added to basic communication the relational skills are key. These are the ability to understand, motivate and communicate at a higher level with others, enabling them to recognise the issues and objectives and understand the space within which they and the organisation are operating. This will need the client to emphasise scenarios and examples so that employees have reference material upon which to understand the basis of the decision for change.

Having given employees a sense of security, or at least a platform from which to identify with the decision to outsource, it is useful to involve them in the strategic thinking. Too often organisations assume their employees will not understand or be interested when the opposite is true. The strategic thinking will help them to identify with the desired state – what are we trying to achieve? Assess the current situation and from that work out the gap analysis for themselves in order to understand the plans and activities required to get to where the organisation needs to be. If this communication starts before the project plans for transition are complete, the value to the project implementation can be immense. Barriers and blockages are removed and employees own ideas can be incorporated resulting in them owning the transition and committing to seeing it through.

The client will require some systemic thinking skills in order to identify and understand the space in which the communications programme is needed. Systemic thinking is at the root of effective problem solving and the ability to create functional teams – whether in the client company or the provider organisation. The ability to do this in a practical and concrete way is probably the most definitive sign of maturity in a leader.

Publicity, ownership and buy-in

The study of group dynamics attempts to understand and improve the nature of human groups and the psychological and social influences associated with groups. The term was first used by Kurt Lewin in 1939 who suggested that one of the key characteristics of a successful group was the level to which people are attracted to it. This cohesiveness when high, allows people to be drawn in and participate and for the group to attain goals and objectives, getting a feeling of self worth, security and identity.

This happens through an understanding of differing maps of the world and maintaining a balance of the points of view of others. In organisations the group view often transcends the views of individuals and this is how cultures evolve. Consensus exerts pressure on individuals and affects communication, attitude and can make success easy or can limit buy-in.

The challenge therefore when communicating change, e.g. the decision to outsource some or all of the Human Resources function, is how to maintain or enhance the structure and attitude of group members while acknowledging the needs for change and difference.

A key aspect in the management of change is the communication strategy adopted by employees (the group members) and those in leadership roles. Some of the areas to take into account will include:

- The knowledge and understanding of the individuals

- The body language and style of the leaders

- The thinking and learning styles of individuals

- The beliefs, values and role identity of all involved.

When communicating the new ways of working, the client will want to maximise the positive impact. There are four influential elements to take into account.

The way people represent concepts and process information. These are derived from preferred use of senses and so language involving seeing, hearing and feeling words should be incorporated into communications strategies. In this way security can be built through use of familiar words.

For example, you will all have been *hearing* comments about changing the way we run our Human Resources department. You may have *seen* visitors in the building recently and this may have caused *feelings* of excitement and expectation.

Varying channels of communication have different uses and strengths. So in addition to the words, some handouts or Powerpoint presentation, even flip chart work to appeal to visual people and some experiential examples to appeal to the kinaesthetics will aid the buy in and maintain rapport. In communicating with anyone, matching their channels of representation can be an important method of building the relationship. We all know people who resist being told what to do but when shown examples the resistance is diminished.

Thinking styles are expressed through varying levels of physiology. Walt Disney described these as *Dreamer*, *Realist* and *Critic*. He suggested that some people need to dream, to imagine what may be, to see the big picture and to start at the end of a project and work backwards. To create new ideas and goals. The *Dreamers* need to represent and widen the concept of the original plan and to orientate towards a longer term future. Questions they may ask include:

- What's the reason for outsourcing?

- What are the potential benefits to employees, customers, business partners, the provider?

- What other possibilities are there?

- What could outsourcing lead to in the future?

The *Realists* have to keep a sense of security, feet on the ground and deal with the art of the possible. Realists want a workable plan and service, focused on procedures and operations. They want detail about what can happen, when and within given resources and how to transform ideas into positive and concrete expressions. Questions they may ask include:

- What is the time frame for the changeover?

- Who are the key players?

- What is the first or next step?

- How do you know when you are making progress?

- What resources do we have to assist in making this change successful?

The third group, the *Critics* need time to knock the concept down, to pick their way through obstacles and barriers, to critique the plans and be listened to. The critic is necessary as a filter and as a stimulus for refinement. These external thinkers will then find a route through that they feel safe with. They will pre-empt scenarios and find missing links. They are not necessarily negative and it is often worth asking them what is the positive intent behind the perceived criticism? Questions they may ask include:

- Who may be positively or negatively affected by the change to outsourcing?

- Why might someone object?

- What are their needs or expectations?

- What is missing?

- Under what circumstances would we not proceed with this project?

Recognising the cues associated with these internal states and thinking styles is a useful skill to focus attention. When communicating with a group or team patterns of physiology and language may be used to match, pace and lead the general thinking style of the whole group.

How often have managers been accused of being on the other side of the mountain while leaving the team down in the valley?

A great metaphor for managing change is for the client to meet the team down in the valley, slowly stroll up the first couple of hills, then gradually walk faster up and down the next few, always returning to some valleys along the route before upping the pace to jogging, running and eventually flying from one mountain top to the next with no need for hills and valleys along the way.

The sooner the organisation meets employees in the valley and starts the stroll, the sooner everyone will fly.

On a macro level, the attitude of an individual is determined by that person's outcome plus his or her attitude. The success of the client will depend on the client's ability to match the needs and perceptions of the group members on a number of different levels including thinking styles, values and role identity. To do this effectively the employees must be allowed to share goals and evidence procedures, to be able to ask the questions about: who, why, where, what, how and when, and the effective communicator will answer all these effectively and honestly along the journey.

In summary, gaining ownership and buy in involves answering the following basic questions:

- What is the larger vision or strategy that the organisation is pursuing?

- What is the relationship between that strategy and the employees?

- How will the strategy be implemented and how will everyone know when it is achieved?

- What are the key tasks and relationships necessary for its success?

- What do I have to contribute to make me feel valued?

The features and benefits, the selling in process

One factor in creating success is the ability to solicit and respond to feedback quickly. The client needs to get in front of his/her employees as quickly as possible during the implementation phase of the outsourcing programme, get feedback and respond by changing or varying the process as quickly as required. The client needs to understand that it's OK to make mistakes as long as learning results from them and that there will be more buy in from employees who see their views being taken into account. It is important for the client to work with the vision and collect up others on the way who see it as well – the diamonds. Too much focus on the worms (the non-believers) will hold the process back.

Factors for successful selling in process

- Clear vision of future.

- Ability to articulate and inspire belief in the vision.

- Ability to second position all stakeholders accurately.

- Effective plan.

- Internal marketing and communications strategy.

- Inspire excitement in the process.

- Visible and transparent results – quick wins.

- Partnership in phasing in – working together with provider.

- Proper allocation of resources: time, money and people.

- Compelling presentations and publicity.

- A team that is credible, qualified, well motivated, balanced.

- Planned exit strategy for client company involvement.

- Reframing challenges and finding positive spin.

- Review, evaluate, learn, review evaluate, learn.

In recent years mergers and acquisitions have become the norm. Employees are becoming more used to themselves or people they know having a change of paymaster while the same work continues. However research shows that if not managed well these transfers have less than a 50:50 chance of success. This is often due to the fact that the key decision makers spend all their time and energy focusing on the strategic and financial implications of the transfer and forget the people element. Even when outsourcing Human Resources activities the focus can all to often be on the process, ignoring the actual people involved.

The worst case scenario is that this leads to sabotage. Management become over-stretched, organisational cultures and styles clash, key people leave, there is increased fear leading to power struggles and reduced communication and eventually the business performance is affected. The saving factors are around planning the extent to which the client and provider want to integrate and the speed at which this is done.

Integration is therefore one of the main challenges. The pre and post transfer stages must be considered in the planning process and a 'people audit' should be carried out before the contracts are signed. Secondments early on in the process can be useful to provide positive and informal feedback on the new employer and the secondee can fell s/he is making a valued and pioneering contribution to the process.

Transferring employees and TUPE

The Transfer of Undertakings (Protection of Employment) Regulations came into effect in 1981. The purpose is to protect the rights of employees where there is a transfer of undertakings of their work to a new employer. There is special protection against dismissal where this happens. The background knowledge and understanding of TUPE is vital for both client and provider, both when the client is transferring work previously done in-house to an outsource provider, or where the contract with one provider is being passed to another.

The important question is about how the undertaking is defined. It is easier when a business is being merged or acquired than when a service contract without tangible assets is changing hands. There are many rules regarding the notification to and consultation with the staff involved and these were amended in 1999 in the Collective Redundancies and Transfer of Undertakings (Protection of Employment) (Amendments) Regulations, which removed the employer's right to choose whether to consult with an existing trade union or to invite affected employees to elect representatives.

Now, if a union is recognised it must be consulted, and there are also provisions regarding the election of appropriate representatives. The penalty for failing to consult was also increased.

What should the supplier be considering?

- The existing manning levels and skill requirements.

- The impact of the outsourcing contract on any recruitment or training needs.

- An assessment of the key players, managers and supervisors.

- Decisions regarding redeployment actions.

- Implementation of appropriate redundancy, retraining and recruitment practices.

- Provision of new management development and training programmes to ensure retention and progression of key players.

There are many ongoing arguments regarding the application of TUPE to competitive tendering. The key case to be referred to is: *Suzen v. Zehnacker Gebaudereinigung Krankenhausservice 1997*, and the decisions made in the European Court of Justice. The Court made it clear that transfer of an activity is not sufficient in itself. Where this ruling is applied it is clear that TUPE will only apply if a change of contractor or service provider involves the transfer of significant assets or a major proportion of the workforce. This can leave the employees without protection. Some tribunals therefore will not accept this.

Case study

Around 300 employees whose jobs were sold to another company without consultation were awarded £250,000 in compensation. An employment tribunal ruled that Company X had taken a 'deliberate decision not to inform and consult with its employees'. The employees returned from their Christmas break to find they had a new employer. Although no employee was made redundant by the sale of the business, the workers did have their pensions and pay review changed.

Another recent development relates to the fact that employees object to the automatic transfer of their contracts of employment. Who owns the employee?

When employees know that the new employer intends to make detrimental and substantial changes to their terms and conditions it can be seen as constructive dismissal. The liability for that dismissal stays with the transferor who cannot limit the liability by pretending ignorance about proposed changes. The best solution is for indemnities to be included in the service contract regarding the liabilities of constructive dismissals.

What will employees be asking themselves?

- Will I keep my job?

- Will I keep the same role?

- Will I get a new boss?

- Will they change my title or status?

- Will my pay change?

- Will my future pay be affected?

- What future plans do they have for my team / department?

- What about my future career?

- Will I be expected to work for other clients as well?

- Can I trust the management?

- Will I have to relocate either workplace or home?

The message regarding TUPE is to seek the best legal advice that can be afforded for each and every transfer. The following summary is offered only as a guide at this time.

Legislation

The obligations in respect of transfers of undertakings stems from European Directives that have been translated into legislation in the UK. The start point is:

Acquired Rights Directive (EEC Council Directive No 77/187).

This has been enacted in the UK by Transfer of Undertakings (Protection of Employment Regulations 1981 (TUPE) and Collective Redundancies & Transfer of Undertakings (Protection of Employment) (Amendment) Regulations 1995.

The EC with a further Council Directive 98/50 has subsequently revised the Acquired Rights Directive, and the UK has until July 2001 to draft and implement revised legislation.

Interpretation of the legislation is by the courts and over the past 20 years quite a number of conflicting decisions have been made, but the intention of the legislation is clear and that is to protect an employee's job and their terms and conditions of employment when a transfer is proposed.

Obligations of the Vendor

1. To identify who will be affected by the transfer.

2. To consult with all persons who are affected (either directly or indirectly) by the transfer. Unless the numbers are very small this has to take the form of arranging the appointment (by secret ballot) of employee representatives.

3. The representatives must be informed of:

    (a) the fact that the relevant transfer is to take place, when, approximately, it is to take place and the reasons for it;

    (b) the legal, economic and social implications of the transfer for the affected employees;

(c) the measures which the employer envisages he/she will, in connection with the transfer, take in relation to the affected employees or, if he/she envisages that no measures will be taken, that fact;

(d) if the employer is the transferor, the measures which the transferee envisages that he/she will take in connection with the transfer in relation to those employees who will become his/her employees on transfer.

4. To ensure that consultations are meaningful and that adequate time is given for representations to be made.

5. To give the purchaser sufficient information in respect of the affected staff's terms and conditions to enable full continuity of employment to successfully transfer.

6. Not to dismiss any employee, in anticipation of, or as a result of the impending transfer. Any such dismissal is automatically unfair and could result in a penalty of up to £50,000 per employee. In cases of discrimination the penalty is unlimited.

Obligations of the purchaser

1. To provide information to the vendor so that the obligation for meaningful consultation can be carried out. The penalty for not holding proper consultations is four weeks' pay per employee affected.

2. To employ all staff who transfer on identical terms and conditions as they previously enjoyed. It is not necessary to write and formally appoint staff it is automatically assumed that they transfer on their previous contract of employment.

3. To be responsible for all liabilities associated with the employees i.e.
   - all existing contractual terms
   - liability for past breaches of contract
   - statutory liabilities
   - personal injury liability
   - profit share or bonus schemes
   - any industrial tribunal cases which arise, even if prior to the transfer.

   NB. Occupational pension obligations do *not* transfer.

4. Not to dismiss any employee of the company as a result of the transfer (post acquisition) unless there is a proper economic, technical or organisational reason for so doing. The maximum penalty is £50,000 per employee.

5. Not to vary the terms of employment of any of the transferees – can be constructive dismissal and is automatically unfair.

6. Any 'Economic, Technical and Organisational' changes can be implemented, provided statutory periods of consultation and due process are followed. An industrial tribunal would require proof that the dismissals were 'fair' (Note – they are not 'automatically unfair'). Penalties for non-consultation, up to 13

weeks pay, additionally the penalty for unfair dismissal is up to £50,000. In the case of discrimination the penalty is unlimited.

Another piece of legislation to take care over is the Disability Discrimination Act and its extensions to small businesses and the rights of people with cancer. People with cancer will now be protected against discrimination from the moment it is diagnosed as being likely to require treatment. Those who have recovered or are in remission are also protected. Evidence has been found of people who are in remission from cancer being sacked or made redundant. Care must therefore been taken in selecting those people and roles for redundancy as a consequential loss as a result of the outsourcing contract.

Project management, timelines and staying on track

Project management skills will include being proactive, coping strategy for multi-roles and ambiguity, long timescales and the ability to take a wide perspective.

The project manager will have to be able to display excellent interpersonal skills. Often outsourcing programmes can impact on internal employees in a way that they feel they have lost something. Interpersonal sensitivity both on the client side and from the supplier is key. Other skills employed will be those of political astuteness, management of groups, conflict resolution, the ability to identify blockers, negotiation and coaching aptitudes. Active listening and the constant and consistent giving, soliciting and receiving of feedback are key.

The project manager must ensure the supplier's project team understands the client's systems and people, are aware of the internal language and jargon, can identify with the client's vision and aspirations, understands the client's business and they are consistently the same people thus building trust and familiarity throughout the transfer process.

Table 4 The difference that makes the difference

Average project teams	Great project teams
• Focus on costs and internal priorities	• Obsessed with client need
• Behaviours based on values of individual members	• Shared values and behaviours centred on client and employees
• Bureaucratic structure	• Common understanding of vision
• Management control	• Flexible roles and responsibilities
• Only financials are measured	• Managers empower others
• No client feedback	• Customer and performance orientated measures
• Traditional infrastructure	• Client needs shaped infrastructure
• Limited focus on learning	• Continuous learning and improvement

Motivation, rewarding sought after behaviours, integrated operating styles

As the unemployment situation reduces and the economy improves both client and provider need to focus on employee retention. Where the provider takes over key knowledge workers s/he will need to understand what motivates them and to link appropriate personal incentives to productivity, performance and retention.

In these days of working partners and parents, co-ordinating leave and childcare can be self defeating if the incentives, e.g. travel and hotel breaks, actually cause the employee an inconvenience.

Whatever route is chosen, the key areas for consideration are changes of culture, management power struggles, fear and anxiety and the loss of key staff. The whole transfer needs to be managed in a positive state with high motivation so that hidden values are realised and the whole operation is synergistic.

Rewards and incentives will need to include:

- review and harmonisation of salary and pay structures;

- appropriateness of base salaries;

- fixed and variable packages;

- the types and numbers of incentives;

- the links of incentives to new performance standards;

- short and long-term incentives;

- retention strategies;

- new performance objectives developed from the outsourcing strategy;

- motivational perks.

Table 5 What makes the inclusive partnership?

Successful integration	Failure
• Faith, trust and hope	• Broken promises
• Communication of vision	• No vision
• Concerns discussed	• Lack of care for individuals
• Respect and credibility	• No respect earned
• Leaders offer support	• No leadership
• Perception of personal benefits	• No personal benefits
• Integrated systems	• Confusion
• Realistic project management	• Lack of planning
• Employee involvements	• Autocratic style
• Systems and reward support the change	• Systems and reward leverage unhelpful behaviours
• Improved incentives	• Incentives reduced

Successful integration centres around five fundamental characteristics:

1. Direction: consistent management of the people, strategic direction and culture.

2. Contribution: defined and measurable productivity and trans-parent performance management systems, with action taken for poor performance.

3. Capability: the skills, knowledge and attitudes employed against job profiles related to client need.

4. Accountability: individual roles and responsibilities related to objectives, organisational vision and clarity and the ease of understanding of the structure.

5. Costs: rewards and benefits packages, training and develop-ment, wealth statements etc.

The current labour market also suggests that retention strategies are key. It is in the interests of client and provider that key employees are kept during the transfer of undertakings as these people will have critical corporate knowledge and understanding of systems vital to ensuring a successful partnership.

Blanket agreements that offer employment to 100% of the employees are being used regularly and add to the feeling of security. In some cases, usually public sector, the employees have a say in how the provider is chosen and sometimes who is chosen. The media pay attention to what is happening and can influence selection based on previous publicity and track record. Once the transfer has been made, providers are designing innovative work environments, career opportunities and focusing on employee satisfaction.

The changing mindset from being a cost when employed by the client to a revenue generating partner can also free up the creativity within the individuals and the focus of their job becomes the mission of the company they are joining. Career development comes as they are then able to get involved in resourcing several accounts.

Critical success factors for integrated operating styles

- Having the right numbers of employees with the skills, knowledge and attitudes to meet the client needs.

- Having the right numbers of managers and team leaders with the skills, knowledge and attitudes to meet the business needs.

- The ability to develop and maintain a committed and motivated workforce.

- The development of clarity of contract requirements and a focus on performance and measurable results.

- The development of a culture committed to quality and continuous improvement.

- A clear focus on added value, savings and client needs.

- The development of the capability to manage change, chaos and complexity effectively.

- The ability to manage costs within contractual agreement.

- To be able to develop and maintain the internal and external contract profile.

- To provide accurate, timely and relevant commercial management information.

- The ability to continually define, refine, focus, update, curtail and amend services in response to client business environment.

The project management activity will develop effectively through continuous linking to the client business strategy, influencing the key opinion formers and decision makers, working with the converted (the diamonds), reducing the blockers (the worms), advertising and celebrating success and continually finding and reframing pressure points.

The integration stage of the outsourcing activity should be long term and never underestimated, where large numbers of employees are involved this can be 12 to 24 months and becomes the spring-board for long terms and sustainable change. Clients looking for a short-term fix take the risk of damaging the organisational culture and expensive repair costs if they do not make the effort to understand the integration and alignment needs. The good plan will manage the aftermath and fallout from the transfer and build confidence, create support and enthusiasm for the new process. This will validate the business case and add stability to the provider base.

The integration phase will be about comparing the duplications, synergies and conflicts between the initial service level agreement and reality. At each review the vision for the future can be revised and the overlaps used to create a positive alignment for each overlap area. The integration team will be made up of both provider and client employees at varying levels of hierarchy and the communication needs of each set of stakeholders must be evaluated so they can be met. Important communication messages will be about how much, how often and when. The key priority should be to reduce chaos and complexity as much as possible and move into the future. It is fundamental that the client provides budgeted resource for communication and training and development at this phase as an investment in the future success of the outsourcing programme.

The obvious disadvantage to using multiple providers instead of a single operator is the management and integration of the overall process. However, often the single operator cannot provide the individual attention that is needed for each process - especially with a first time client who has old systems and methodology in place. The challenge of dealing with the implementation or solution finding in many complex functions at the same time will prove too complicated. An additional cost, but maybe more of an investment, will be to outsource the co-ordination of the process to a consultant or broker who acts as the One Stop Shop for the client and maintains a strategic overview of the new programmes.

Case study

The company in question consolidated internal support functions in a new 'shared services' division which was then located away from the main sites of the operational environment. The Human Resources activity covered the whole spectrum of the Human Resource function.

The first decision was whether to consolidate the HR activities or outsource them. Due to the continuing changes in tax and employment legislation and increasing workload as a result, the case for outsourcing was growing. The internal function also had a home grown computerised administration system, which was creaking. Outsourcing offered the chance to get up-to-date systems without capital expenditure, reduced internal programming requirements while eliminating the need for expensive staff briefing, training and ongoing development.

The company used an outsourcing consultant to define their needs and following a recommendation to outsource the whole of Human Resources the consultant recommended a provider who then assembled a specialist project team from the varying specialist areas to implement the outsourcing agreement.

The primary objectives were to improve the level of employee satisfaction with the HR processes, provide a broader perspective of service and functionality to the programmes, consolidate the system under a single computerised management system and keep costs down. In addition best practice would be sought in each area. The objective was to provide enhanced benefits for the company and the employees at the same time, and to adopt an approach, which would give a better service than could ever be realised within the internal organisation.

The first challenge was to define the requirements for the separate areas and to work with the managers to define what were the success criteria for each. The top five requirements were matched to the provider's list of best practices and in some cases the client's current practices were preferred.

The contract was then developed over time providing for a system of incentives and penalties that would deliver best practice, best overall service and customer satisfaction. In addition to the usual measurements of error rate, call waiting, response times, problem solving timescales, the contract focused on adding value. The measurements for the bigger issues included incentives.

Overall there were more than 30 service level measures in five areas. The more creative ones related to the provider's requirements to provide ideas and recommendations for service improvements based on their operating experiences on a quarterly basis. There were financial incentives for improving satisfaction and reducing costs and measurement includes employee satisfaction surveys.

The provider developed a corrective action matrix with four levels of severity. For the most serious action types there could not be more than two occurrences in twelve months or the contract could be terminated without penalty. There could be no more than four incidents in twelve months of the next most severe action with resolution required within fifteen days. The entire process is tracked on a performance matrix and 80% of the reports are available from standard systems. There is a clear balance between incentives and penalties with a financial risk for sub-standard service and the same amount available for incentives.

The provider – in this case Hewitt Associates – is enthusiastic about the arrangement. Hewitt Associates have seen their clients evolve from organisations eager for 'rescue' from benefits administration problems to organisations that demand clear and convincing evidence of benefits from outsourcing arrangements. By putting some of their revenues and risk and sharing in the rewards of cost reduction and creative service improvements, Hewitt is sure that their clients will provide them with clear and convincing evidence that will be useful with other potential outsourcing clients. This case study has helped them identify the value adding services they are able to deliver to prospective clients.

The client anticipates that reducing their HR team by 75%, improving employee satisfaction and providing significantly expanded services in addition to dramatic improvements in service will have direct correlation to customer satisfaction and will impact the bottom line. Both client and provider expect the relationship to grow stronger as both recognise the benefits of WIN:WIN.

CHAPTER 7

The future

Predicting the future

When reviewing the future for the Human Resources outsourcing activities it makes sense to review the future of the Human Resources function. It could be debated that the current work of HR today in becoming internal consultants focused on organisational design, performance management, creative implementation of employment legislation etc. is taking the function into even less tangible areas and that the future will see a return to centralisation and control. That having passed through the era of freelance and contract workers, companies will return to a need for security through employment as team leaders and managers find the flexible structures too unfettered and complex to deal with and the uncertainty causes them to demand transactional Human Resources with measurements and administration core to the new systems and processes.

The future is probably not that easily predictable. The future of HR will emanate from the future of organisations and the vagaries of living in a global society, which is even now dealing with information and knowledge management, intellectual and human capital and the many other ingredients of organisational transformation. What we can be sure of is that every organisation will manage it in what appears the most appropriate way for them, that sociological changes will cause changes to work patterns and that traditional employees will be more careful in choosing how they work rather than responding to circumstance. This is already evidenced by the under-25-year-olds today who are very clear about what they want and what they will or will not put up with.

The possible employment scenarios will vary from one where people turn up to carry out a task related activity, are only interested in the job for what it delivers in terms of reward to finance other areas of life, and have very little expectation of commitment both from and to the employer. This role will require the base line administrative support of the HR function. One lesson that HR has learned over the years is that automating work does not necessarily improve performance. Unless the content and context of the work is reviewed it may mean that the quantity of irrelevant work is simply done faster. The first question to ask therefore is to inquire whether the work should be done at all and the second would be to continue use of the self-service activity and leave the area with low transactional support on an as needed basis accessed through contact centre by computer or telephone.

The second variant will be those of project workers, either interim or trouble shooters, who turn up, throw themselves heart and soul into the role, gaining job satisfaction in the short term. The main role of HR here is recruitment, record administration, training and development, compensation and end of assignment bonusing arrangements. This will require more of a generalist account management response, a person who has knowledge of the business unit and generalist HR understanding, who can deal with operational issues quickly and easily.

The third variant will be those of individual contracts, where employees will negotiate their terms and conditions, roles and responsibilities thus selling themselves and their capabilities to the organisation which most closely meets their aspirations. The Human Resources activity here would be complex and multi-transactional and demand a specialist response from a professional well versed in the given area, its application to corporate strategy and the ability to give a quality commercial response.

This final scenario links to the customer centric role to be adopted by Human Resources practitioners, this role being based on the psychological contract, the varying content of job and varying needs and desires of individuals, thus the coaching, consulting and sales roles become key. All three scenarios are driven by service excellence, composed of low cost, efficiency and effectiveness and maximum up-to-date information available with a rapid response.

What will have to change for sure is the profile and credibility of Human Resources. The current habit of getting HR involved in the implementation of projects over which they have no power and authority and which may cause them a major professional values clash, but which they are bullied to doing through a lack of voice on the Board, will have to cease. They are currently asked to become 'business partners' but there are mixed messages around this façade. For sure Human Resources professionals will become leaders and full partners, committing to the greater mission of the organisation and having the power to hold onto standards of behaviour and the organisational values in order to get there. The key to this is the confidence and spirit of the professionals. At an 'HR Intensive', a meeting of senior HR Directors, the constant theme of the meeting was around the words – 'I can't …, I'm not allowed to …' The author's repost was 'who said?', only to discover that the meeting attendees were playing to limiting beliefs or self-imposed assumptions. The advice – just get on and do what you believe in until it is questioned, make sure you have some quick wins, you are the guardians of employment legislation, what is the worst thing that can happen if you mess up?

The Human Resources function of the future

- Strategic HR planning and implementation.

- Organisational design and structure.

- Human Resources systems and process and the management of the co-dependency.

- The management of personal, team and organisational transformation.

- Employer branding, managing the values driven two way contract.

- Identity and alignment, managing the integration of employee and employer.

- Building a credible image; internal and external networking, knowledge management, marketing and PR.

- Managing inclusiveness. Building the trust and integrity to work in a partnership to achieve common goals.

When reviewing the needs of the future, the outsourcing scene may appear to change. This will lead to the organisation to beware of putting too many eggs in one basket or having lengthy contracts without break clauses. For sure the future is a mix of insourced and outsourced services with some reporting to others outside the Human Resources function. Indeed, the structure of the entire organisation could be impacted upon with the setting up of a role linked to the negotiation of outsourced service provision, looking after information technology, finance, treasury, general administration, security, facilities management, catering, telesales, customer service, contact centres, logistics fulfilment, etc.

Some research is showing that the Human Resources outsourcing industry is becoming one of intense competition, fragmented with a lack of uniformity among suppliers. The service offerings and market propositions are starting to differ greatly, barriers to entry are low and the number of entrants is growing as large companies make people redundant and allow them to then run the outsource contract – thus encouraging the growth of small businesses with high client dependency.

As clients become more sophisticated their demands will be more qualitative and the fragmentation will decrease as providers have to tender against more highly defined criteria.

The number of outsource providers will explode as organisations challenge every internal overhead and whether their strategy is to add value or reduce cost, every operating function will come under the spotlight. Those people currently employed in roles such as Director of Shared Services, Human Resources Director etc will become Resourcing Directors and a key part of their function will be to manage multiple outsourcing relationships. In a bid to whittle this down, providers will become brokers of more generic services so that the Resourcing Directors have to deal with fewer contacts – this places enormous demands on outsourcing account managers in terms of knowledge, thus providing a new career route for the MBA type of individual who will need to have a clear strategic understanding about how organisations function.

So far much of the outsourcing phenomena has resulted from the interest of the 'big 5' consulting firms. This will change. Outsourcing originated from the USA because of its service-based economy. Now that the UK operating base has changed from manufacturing to service, the concept will take off. The consulting firms can be see as idealistic and unable to implement the strategies they have recommended so the outsourcing providers of the future will come from more generalist and operational arenas but not forgetting the need to be able to provide expert advice and proven track records. Those companies with a background in providing outsourced services in catering, cleaning, security services, document management etc. are well placed to switch their focus to the professional and administrative services to facilitate the strategic objectives of an organisation.

The importance of regular client review has been emphasised elsewhere in this book. The end of year review is a more strategic approach. It should be timed to follow the strategic planning, business planning and budgeting processes of the client and is an opportunity to review the medium and long term health of the partnership. It is a time for 'blue sky thinking', a time for creative and inspirational planning, for dreaming, indeed for 'getting out of the box'.

'*If you do what you always do you get what you always got!*' One of the dangers with outsourcing Human Resources relationships is that the communication can become routine and transactional as it takes on the characteristics of many of the tasks involved. This is at a time in our economic revolution when the people side of the business has become of such vital significance to success that the business world will never be the same again.

It is only by embracing change, complexity and chaos that organisations will survive and by living in the moment that the human brain is able to cope with the speed of development. In this new world the traditional roles and responsibilities, hierarchies, predictable planning cycles, self justification, exhaustion and burn-out, bureaucracy, obligation, external referencing and dependency disappear. These are replaced by flexible and transformational team working and living in the moment. New behaviours based on harmony, playfulness, creativity, internal referencing, use of intuition and spontaneity replace old school inconsistencies and knowledge is available freely and immediately in real time – it's what companies do with it that makes the difference. To quote David Vice, CEO at Northern Telecom: '*In the future there will be two types of companies, the quick and the dead*'.

The end of year review must take this into account. The real value adding of outsourcing the Human Resources activities is the ability to objectively harness the 'people power' from within an organisation and create the environment for energy and inspiration to abound. '*An internet year is three months*', therefore, the concept of end of year review is a metaphor for a place in time where it is appropriate for all concerned to take stock.

The providers of the future will align systems and process with the intuitive and spiritual sides of the relationship. They will influence their clients through their beliefs, values and behaviours, systems and process never were a differentiator. The providers who succeed will constantly be state of the art and at the cutting edge of continuous and innovative improvement.

The key to outsourcing Human Resources in the future will be to put the management and motivation of people back where it firmly belongs – in the hands of the people. Self management, awareness and responsibility will abound. Individuals will not only be responsible for keeping their own records up-to-date, they will take these with them from employer to employer. The Government is putting more and more responsibility onto employers for tax collection, this will be passed on. Every individual will have his/her personal records, which include up-to-date CV, personal development records, holidays and absenteeism, financial status, purchasing history, property ownership. The days of the personal database are coming. There is no point to duplication, the only person who owns this information is the individual and a world is rapidly approaching where the individual will sell his or her updated records to those who have an interest. This alone suggests that the days of self service or intranet based Human Resources record keeping are numbered and that the future suggests an integrated database management system. This takes on a whole new concept of Customer Relationship Management.

It is the quality of alliance between client and outsource provider that will get to these changes and develop strategies to take on board and enhance new concepts without protectionism. In the new economy successful organisations whether clients or providers (and that's a great debate because the relationship can be co-dependant and work both ways) are about fulfilling dreams. Customers are workers, external customers, consumers and '*everyone we touch*', and the successful client and provider will debate the coping mechanisms required to maintain uniqueness while managing the system with the greatest flexibility. It is those who take the risk, break the rules, do it differently who will succeed. It is not sufficient to satisfy expectation. Every day there must be an element of surprise, of innovation, and every opportunity to change, refine and revise must be exploited.

Already there is a focus on work/life balance. In some areas this is moving towards getting a life instead of work. The days of portfolio working where individuals have more than one job are upon us and for many, work is now a series of projects. This gives individuals more control over how they live their lives, and more freedom to be the people they were born to be. The challenge for organisations is to harness the productivity that comes from this freedom, to unlearn and forget the procedural ways of working almost as soon as they are learned, to do away with intellectual analysis and reflection which slows down achievement as it causes us to compete with like minded organisations, and create a future where response is immediate and risky, emotional and emanates from an innate desire and commitment to achieve something worth having.

The successful outsource provider of the future will insist that the client project team is made up of the customers of the service, a cross section of people within the organisation, the people who really know what successful service provision would look like. This provider will understand that s/he is selling a way of being, which has little to do with price, measurement or performance and more to do with providing a springboard of support, freedom, independence, affection and caring from within which people can grow the performance they need to secure their own and their organisation's futures.

Brand management, both for the client and provider, will be of the utmost importance and will be measured on emotional values albeit by more focused organisations. Knowledge-based companies are already moving ahead in the business to business and business to consumer markets. The support of people in these roles will demand co-ordination, partnering and leadership, rather than the traffic warden mentality of Human Resources in the past. The successful players will have a firm, focused yet value adding orientation towards the future.

The 'solutions centre' approach will be key to the future. This will be the strategic consulting and expert knowledge driver that transforms organisations. It may be the transformation of the Human Resources profession as there will be no room for operational generalists at this level.

Experts from compensation, management development, industrial relations, media and communications as well as the legal people will be employed as futurists to take organisations forward. These people will have no interest in reporting to the Board on the number of sick days taken in the dim recesses of last month, instead they will be in a planning unit working on competitive edge strategies. They could be partners in an outsourced professional services firm, they could be senior employees within the organisation, without doubt they will be the strategic decision makers who pass the decisions onto project teams for implementation. These people will be at the forefront of organisational development, consulting with and influencing business partners in terms of commercial growth, they will be the knowledge providers, the re-engineering team, the transformational change leaders.

The output of the Human Resources function whether insourced, outsourced or co-sourced, will provide the sense of emotional stability that human beings need in order for being human or 'humanness' to maintain and sustain competitive edge in the economy of the future. As collective disputes come back into fashion, the economy changes and recruitment shortages bite the management of equality and diversity become a core focus especially in the public sector where outsourcing has swept the board in the last few years. As a result many Human Resources professionals now work outside the main employing organisation and can be just as influential as those within.

As the Human Resources outsourcing activity grows, more and more models will become virtual instead of bricks and mortar. Industry growth will triple over the next couple of years with more and more menus of options becoming the standard offering, albeit these will be tailored to individual employees requirements as well as their employers. Global coverage will be the norm for the best providers who will become brokers and distribution channels for the specialist service companies.

Web-based models such as Motivano and Dr. Benefits will provide a cost effective mechanism for managing individual choice on a daily basis, backed up by contact service centres. These will offer a higher return on investment than traditional models. As previously discussed added value comes from the removal of some of the intimidating internal Human Resources contact and therefore trust builds through improved employee relations and perceived improved privacy.